LIST OF ILLUSTRATIONS

Page numbers in black refer to the Notes on the Plates; those in red refer to the gravure illustrations

CONTENTS

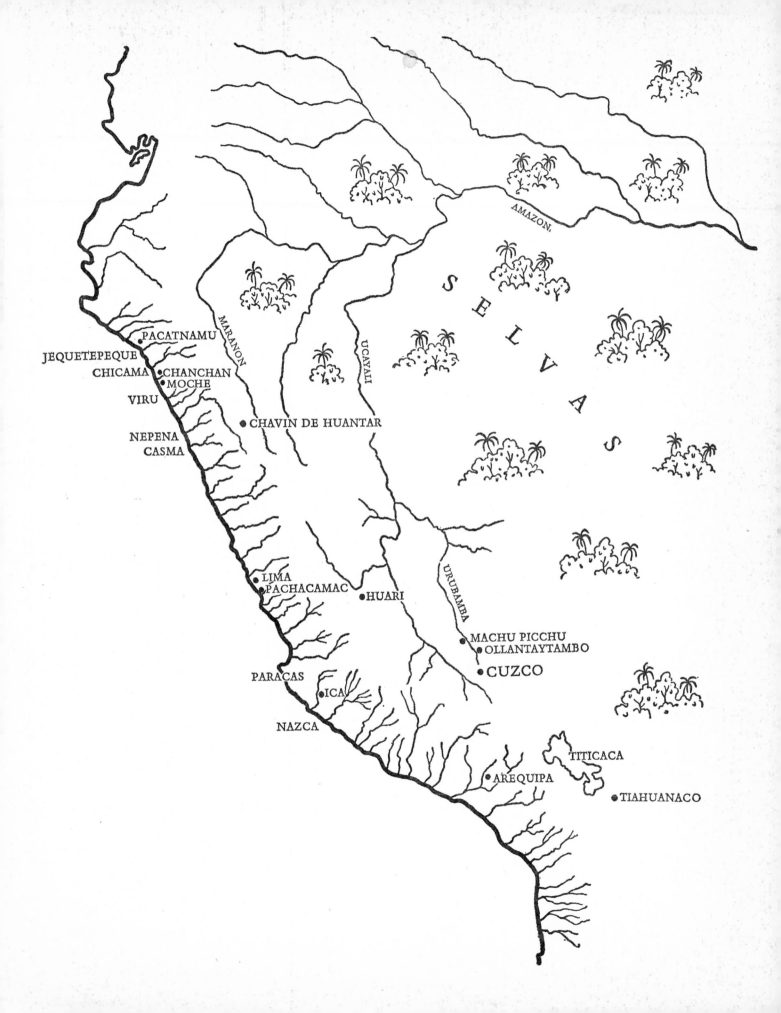

JEQUETEPEQUE
PACATNAMU
CHICAMA • CHANCHAN
MOCHE
VIRU
NEPENA
CASMA

MARANON

CHAVIN DE HUANTAR

UCAYALI

AMAZON

S E L V A S

LIMA
PACHACAMAC
HUARI

URUBAMBA

MACHU PICCHU
OLLANTAYTAMBO
CUZCO

PARACAS
ICA

NAZCA

TITICACA
AREQUIPA
TIAHUANACO

INTRODUCTION

Peru is the land of the Inca, of their temples and fortresses, their palaces and highways. But it is also the land of far older ruined cities and pyramids, whose origins had already become obscured in the darkness of a thousand years when in the late fifteenth and early sixteenth centuries the Inca Huayna Capac ruled over the greatest empire of ancient America. Thus ancient Peru reveals not only the Inca, but a history of over two thousand years ending with the arrival of Pizarro in 1532. All but a tenth of this history is still imperfectly known. Yet even this period of two thousand years covers only the advanced Inca and pre-Inca cultures of the Central Andes and the adjacent western coastlands. What came before has only recently begun to emerge, gradually, from the obscurity of prehistory.

No script is known from ancient Peru, and this absence of written records largely explains our ignorance of its history before the Spaniards arrived. What is known derives from oral tradition among the indigenous inhabitants, much of which is inconsistent. Of the well-known *quipu*, or counting devices of knotted string, those which have been preserved in graves were used, according to the researches of Erland Nordenskiöld, for astrological calculations; other *quipu* which later chroniclers record as having been used for keeping a wide variety of records in Inca times have not survived. The absence of writing in ancient Peru has surprised many who admire the advanced development of its cultures. But it is too easily forgotten that especially in early times a historical record as we understand the phrase was not to be expected, nor would it have been considered. Events had a meaning primarily in a magico-religious sense. For recording what was magic or religious there was a sacred writing, a type of hieroglyphic system composed of symbols ordered or combined together, which finds its richest expression in weaving. This is a hieratic 'script' which effectively expresses the author's interpretation of events; but it is far from what we need to be able to reconstruct the sequence of events in the history of ancient Peru.

In the absence of historical sources for the pre-Spanish period we have to rely on oral tradition which was written down by Spanish and Indian chroniclers after the Spanish conquest. And we have to attempt, especially for the centuries on which tradition throws no light, to discover the past through archaeological excavation. Archaeological fieldwork predominates over all other methods of enquiry. In the words of A. L. Kroeber, 'Associations within graves remain and probably will long remain one of our most important channels to the sharper understanding of Peruvian history' (1956, p. 339).

For archaeologists the coast of Peru is a paradise matched only by Egypt. Owing to the extreme dryness of the soil in these areas where rain is scarcely known, much that was deposited in graves one or two thousand years ago, or buried under fallen adobe walls, has been preserved as in an air-conditioned atmosphere: pottery, textiles, gold, silver, copper, bronze, wood, precious stones, shell-fish and crops, especially maize. From graves in the southern valleys (the Nazca region) colourful cloaks have been found which are quite new in appearance although they are from five hundred to a thousand years old. From the most southerly valley, Las Trancas, I have excavated maize which was about twelve hundred years old; some of the grain was later planted in my garden where it germinated and grew into plants three feet high, though they bore no corn.

For over a hundred years the archaeological wealth of Peru has been increasingly exploited, by *huaqueros* (treasure-seekers), although they have been partially restrained by the action of the Peruvian government, and by archaeologists. It is scarcely a century since earlier complexes began to be discerned, anonymous for the most part beside the dazzling name of the Inca, until they were identified and named by archaeologists. The outlines and forms of previously unknown cultures became clearer. These were cultures with a passionate power for religious portrayal, which the art of the Inca cannot match in either vigour or variety.

From a study of ancient Peruvian art in all its aspects three general styles have been distinguished (see chart on pp. 16, 17), the so-called 'type styles' which in their respective periods extended throughout the Central Andean region and the corresponding stretch of coast. The Chavín style *(160, 161)* is assigned to the centuries before the birth of Christ, the Tiahuanaco style *(172–177, 201)* to the second half of the first millennium AD, and the Inca style to the century before the arrival of the Spaniards. Only the Inca style corresponds with a defined cultural region (which however included several peoples). The two others, and especially the Chavín style, were not the expression of political dominion, but mark the spread of strong religious influences throughout the Central Andean region. Little is known about the origin of these two great religious movements. It is an unsolved problem whether the Tiahuanaco style originated as a movement from the site of South America's most famous ruins at Tiahuanaco itself (south-east of Lake Titicaca) or from Huari (near Ayacucho, north-west of Cuzco). Still less is it known whether the more sinister and passionate tranports of the Chavín movement developed at the type-site of Chavín de Huantar on the eastern slopes of the Cordillera Blanca in central Peru. The Chavín style presents the greater puzzle since what preceded it is still largely unknown.

Between the universal type styles of the chronological framework lie regional styles belonging to specific areas (see chart pp. 16, 17), such as the Mochica style in the north *(67, 71–80, 91–95, 128–136)* and the Nazca style in the south *(185–189)*. Both of these are assigned to the third-sixth centuries AD, thus falling between the Chavín and Tiahuanaco horizon styles. Mochica developed from the so-called Gallinazo style of the first three or four centuries AD, with its primitive-looking pottery. From the Nazca style in the south apparently developed two Paracas styles which take their name from the Paracas peninsula; it was here that the Peruvian archaeologist Julio Tello discovered the cemeteries which have since become famous. The more recent, the Paracas Necropolis style, is exemplified in embroidered shrouds which have excited international interest among collectors; in its later stages this style ran concurrently with the Nazca style. The older, the Paracas Cavernas style, known less from textiles than from its distinctive pottery which was painted after firing, can be assigned roughly to the first and second centuries AD.

These dates are approximations as are almost all those I give here and in the charts. Even the figures from radiocarbon-14 dating cannot be exact since we must allow for a possible margin of error of at least a hundred years on either side of the calculated date. However it is a great achievement to be able to fix the probable date of a vase or a textile to within two or three hundred years, and the C-14 method was an important step forward.

It should not then be a disappointment if the figures on the charts still need revision. The relative chronology of ancient Peru, that is the relative sequence of the numerous ancient cultures known to us today, is in its main outlines much more exactly determined than it was fifty years ago. When it becomes apparent that the Mochica style is divided into early, 'classical' and late forms, it will be seen that the chronological limits of this culture tend to expand on a concise chart. But to produce a detailed chart showing all of the ever increasing number of known general and particular styles would be not only cumbersome, but to those not entirely familiar with the archaeology of Peru it would prove confusing.

I do not intend to give a complete presentation of Peruvian archaeology. What I should like to do is to engage the interest of the reader, as though he were visiting the sites, in a series of excavations carried out under my direction on expeditions in 1931/32, 1937–39, 1953/54 and 1962/63. At the same time I should like to show something of the setting in which the archaeological finds were made, and at least to outline some of the characteristics of the peculiar and still largely veiled spiritual world revealed by the graves and their contents as well as by other aspects of the material. An unbiased observer will be struck by the diversity of many of the finds. On a first approach to the Peruvian mind through a general presentation of ancient Peruvian culture, like that set out here in the plates, the impression of its essential heterogeneity is paramount. To illustrate the contrasts one may take the portrait head in Mochica style *(158, 159)* and the trophy head from Sechín *(171)*; or the humming-bird vase *(189)* found with a decapitated body; or the unusual figurines *(120)* and the head reminiscent of an Early Greek goddess *(117)*, both from the Pampa de Tecapa; not to mention the trophy heads from Cahuachi *(191)* belonging to a culture complex closely related to that of grave II at Cahuachi *(180–183)*, in which was found (amongst the material used to fill in the grave) a colourful little needlework butterfly and a lock of black hair bound with thread.

This kaleidoscopic array illustrates the formality of life in ancient Peru, of life lived under the threat of the gods. Nothing is intrinsically beautiful or good; it can only be correct, and what is correct is what is willed by the gods and the magical powers of the insubstantial world. This wins the blessing of the gods. But there is also their severity, and it behoves men to regulate their lives in accordance with the portents of the gods and the all-pervading magic. By magic and charms man may ward off disaster and assure his survival.

Trophy heads, for example, were used to bring harvests and preserve the sacrificer in a calamitous world, while the sacrificial victim was cast down. In the context of these times it would be mistaken to see anything loving or affectionate in the embroidered butterfly or decorated lock of hair. Magic is worked with human hair, and in ancient Peru the butterfly was perhaps connected with thoughts of graves and the other world and not of a dead person transformed. Transformation of a dead man into a bird is however not infrequently represented by clay models. And it is directly symbolized in the Nazca region at Huayurí, where a bird's wing was bound to the hand of a mummy with the fingers overlain by feathers, so as to make them appear transformed.

As for the painted humming-bird associated with the beheaded figure, Eduard Seler has already surmised that in ancient times the humming-bird was considered a sort of god of Spring or fertility god, since it disappeared in autumn to return in the spring, when the rivers flowed again and the crops began to grow.

The belief that life was subject to the blessing or anger of the gods and the atmosphere of magic persisted for the people of the Inca empire, when the sacrifice of men and children was still practised in times of great danger or need to preserve the realm.

Throughout the history of ancient Peru the manner of life of the people was bound up with that of their ancestors, who were looked to for blessings on the fields and for the preservation of the living. The dead in their graves were more richly equipped than the living. Between the world of the dead and the world of the living there was a magical and spiritual coexistence. The belief that the living could entreat for the helpful intervention of the dead finds expression in a variety of ways in the graves – in their plans, in the placing of the body and in the offerings – according to the kinship or tribe of the dead person. One of the tasks of the archaeologist is to distinguish between grave types, and between the cultures characterized by them.

Excavations along the northern coast are concerned chiefly with the Mochica culture and its art, partly in a pure form, as at Huaca Campana in the Chicama valley (128–136), and partly intermixed with the so-called Gallinazo culture and a late Chavín style (62–97). In the desert cities of Jatanca and Tecapa (104–122) many of the northern styles, ranging from the most familiar to the almost unknown and from the earliest to the latest, are encountered. On the southern coast my excavations at Locarí revealed the second of the type styles, the Tiahuanaco style (172–177), as well as the early Nazca style (185), partly mixed with the contemporary or slightly older Paracas Necropolis style (188 below, 189). Further excavations produced numerous finds which are earlier than the Tiahuanaco style encountered on the coast. I classified my finds as the Morro style (178–184). This style and the corresponding culture may be characterized as related successors to the Nazca style, but with strong new cultural influences which however show nothing epigonal. From among the late styles of the thirteenth to fifteenth centuries in the north we encountered at Pacatnamú the Chimú style, which persisted even into the fifteenth century which was the period of the Inca and of the decline of the Chimú state.

My studies in architectural history were concerned in the north with the pyramids and terraces of Pacatnamú (52–57), the buildings of the desert cities of Jatanca and Tecapa (104–109, 114–116) and finally with the far earlier ruined cities of Quisque (164–166), Sechín (167–171) and Cerro Blanco (162, 163), all of which are overshadowed by Chavín and the Chavín phenomenon, which must have begun centuries before the birth of Christ. I also carried out comparative research on the two great Moche pyramids (145–149).

In the southern highlands I studied chiefly the buildings of the Cuzco region, i.e. archaeological material from the last centuries before the Conquest (220–233, 236, 237, 268–301). These remains, which are peculiar to the southern Andean region, are concentrated on sacred cliffs and in caves and must have persisted well into the first millennium AD (234, 235, 238–267). The Titicala rock (304) which is situated on the Isla del Sol in Lake Titicaca, also belongs to this Cuzco group.

Travelling through the highlands would not be devoid of interest even if there were no antiquities. The surroundings of the monuments have remained virtually unchanged for centuries. Among the vast mountain ranges modern roads appear as thin and often sinuous lines. The population of the region, too, is basically unchanged in so far as it derives from the Indian mountain peasants, i.e. the majority of the inhabitants of the high valleys around Cuzco *(212, 214–219)*. Present-day clothes moreover are still based on styles of Spanish colonial times. The poncho or woollen cloak *(214–217)*, however, to judge from its shape, is not derived from the Inca period when only a woollen coat fastened at the side or a shirt was worn. By contrast the entire ornamentation of the poncho does go back to pre-Spanish times. Up to the time of my visit to the Cuzco region in 1938 this decoration was preserved in all its full and colourful richness, and it would be most rewarding to record the Indian designations of the motifs and the meaning of the ornamentation as it is still understood, before these last traditions from Inca times fall into oblivion. A poncho 'topography' is also urgently required, showing the distribution of the many poncho styles according to their decoration. My wife and I made some preliminary studies through enquiries, photographic records and numerous colour drawings of costume, as well as by research into weaving techniques.

The Indian peasants of the valleys around Cuzco are certainly descendants of the inhabitants of the central region of the Inca empire in the centuries before the arrival of the Spaniards. Only in some remote eastern valleys does it appear that the migration of herdsmen has produced any significant population movement back and forth in the period since colonial times.

INCA ROADS

Evidence of Inca tracks on the Isla del Sol led us to undertake later studies of the famous Inca roads which are described by all the Spanish chroniclers. The long-distance highways of the Inca empire are the most accomplished technical achievement of ancient America, according to Georg Friederici whose original research (1925, vol. I, p. 174) on the subject I have followed. The Inca empire would have been unthinkable without these highways, just as the highways would be unthinkable without the organization of the empire. Throughout western South America, in the Andes and on the coast, from Ecuador through Peru down into Chile, remnants of important roads are encountered, and they are all in general similar. Wherever it is possible the roads are dead straight, through deserts and mountain ranges, bogs and lakeland. From eighteen to twenty-eight feet wide and flanked by walls, these are roads such as were not known in Europe between the time of the Romans and Napoleon. The *caminos reales del Inca,* the royal highways of the Inca, run in two parallel arteries, along the coast and in the mountains, linked by a series of transverse roads. The mountain highway ran from the northern border of the empire on the river Ancasmayu (not far from the southern frontier of present-day Colombia) to southern Chile, a distance of nearly 4,000 miles. The coast highway crossed numerous valley 'oases'; the total length of this highway system amounted to over 6,000 miles. At intervals of between twelve and twenty miles rest-houses were built for travellers, who were predominantly officials or troops. At wider intervals there were in addition depots for military units on the march, where equipment and supplies could be replenished. The highways indeed served primarily for the administration and defence of the far-reaching empire.

The roads also made possible an outstanding news service, with relays of couriers always on the alert at post houses two miles or less apart. According to the reliable chronicler Bernabé Cobo, writing at the time of the Conquest, a message and answer could be transmitted in twelve days between Cuzco and Quito, a return distance of some 2,800 miles. And it should not be forgotten that the roads ran over rough mountains, snowy plateaux and stony deserts and through forests with thorny thickets, as we are told by Cieza de León, one of the most trustworthy of the chroniclers. Nonetheless the great speed of the couriers was constantly maintained, and they are reputed to have been faster than the Spanish horses and mules which followed, achieving more in one day than these animals could in three. Neither storms nor other contingencies could hinder the couriers, even in the wildest stretches of the route. And as one runner set off, another would come on duty in his place. For the rapid communication of important news and orders there was (according to Garcilasso) a special signal service using smoke signals by day and fires by night. These signal stations were sited so as to be seen from afar. A permanent watch was kept to receive and transmit messages. Garcilasso writes that the signal service was capable of sending messages over distances as great as 1,500–2,000 miles in the space of two or at the most three hours.

The highway system was built in the fifteenth century. The project, which was unprecedented for the time, must have originated with the great reformer and law-giver Pachacutec Yupanqui (c. 1400–48). The plan was carried out by his son Tupac Yupanqui (1448–82) and grandson Huayna Cápac (1482–1529). Cieza de León names Huayna Cápac as the builder of the highways:

Near Huilcas Huaman I saw three or four roads. Once by mistake I set off on one of them, thinking it to be the one at present in use. One of these roads is named after Pachacutec, the other after Yupanqui. But the road which is used at the present time, and which will remain in use for ever, is the one which Huayna Cápac ordered to be built. It reaches the river Ancasmayu in the north and to the south stretches over much of what we today call Chile, a total length of over 1,200 leagues [c. 6,250 miles].

When the ruler decided that one of these famous roads should be built few commands were necessary. Official overseers journeyed through the provinces and determined the route, and workmen carried out the work of completing the section they were charged with. In this way a province would build the road within its boundaries from its own resources and with its own manpower, and in a short time it would be ready. Other provinces would do the same so that when it was necessary long sections of the road, or its whole length, could be built simultaneously.

Cieza adds that such a feat was possible thanks solely to the order bestowed on the realm by the Inca.

Ever since the downfall of the Inca empire these great roads have excited the admiration of European travellers. In the sixteenth century, the century of the Conquest, Cieza de León declared that the Roman roads of the Iberian peninsula did not compare with those of the Inca, and added 'Charles V, in all his splendour, would not be in a position to carry out such a work'.

Agustin de Zárate compares the Inca roads with the Seven Wonders of the Old World, to which they may even be superior. Alexander von Humboldt vividly describes his encounter with some of them:

On the Andean pass between Alausí and Loxa, which is called Páramo del Assuay and at 14,568 ft is almost as high as Mont Blanc, we had great difficulty in getting our heavily laden mules across the boggy ground of the Pullal plateau. Yet nearby our eyes were fixed on the magnificent remains of an Inca road, twenty feet wide and running for a distance of more than a league. The road had a solid foundation and was paved with well-cut dark-brown trap porphyry. Nothing I have seen among the fine Roman roads of Italy, Spain or the south of France was more imposing than these works of the ancient Peruvians.

This almost incomparable highway system, however, was not created from nothing by the Inca. There must have been lines of communication in western South America before the Inca dominion. According to tradition this would have been especially true during the period of the Chimú state, which covered a great part of northern Peru and was conquered about 1450 by the Inca army despite a vigorous defence. Its centre and capital was the town of Chan-Chan (151), near present-day Trujillo. Chimú is the most interesting of the numerous pre-Inca states of ancient Peru and appears to have been highly organized. For the most part, however, in archaeological and general interest it has been and will tend to be eclipsed by the Inca empire, which has come to be credited with the accomplishments of all the states it overthrew. As a result it appears that the Inca people is the essence and embodiment of all political order, even though the Inca really imported their institutions from other lands and combined them into their own state structure. The strength of the Inca and of their officials lay in their talent for organization, and in their ability to recognize what was useful in newly incorporated territories, to adopt it without hesitation and to develop it further for their own profit. Without the Inca, highways of the sort the Spaniards still admired in the sixteenth century would certainly never have been built. But we should not underestimate the very important contribution of non-Inca peoples to the Inca culture.

General adoption by the Inca of successful earlier practices is found in the irrigation systems and cultivation terraces so essential to life in Peru. In the arid climate which Peru's coastal region enjoyed at the time of the high cultures a concentration of population depended on bringing water to the fields and on terracing, a system which inhabitants of the Andes had brought to perfection. Artificial irrigation was an essential element of Inca life, as it had been in its component states, though it could not have been maintained throughout the vast empire without its roads. These great works built by communal labour were dependent on each other and on the state's power in general.

The coastal region of Peru is almost without rain. All the water for cultivation comes down in the rivers from the Western Cordillera (its snowfields and glaciers are visible from passing ships on clear days). Ever since man has inhabited the coast water has been directed from the rivers along countless large and small channels *(acequias)* into the fields. Where the land is irrigated it is desert no more and the soil bears rich harvests. Thus through the bare hills and desert plain *(37, 38)* wind the fertile valley 'oases', marked by the bright green of the crops and the darker green of the river forests, or *montes*. The valleys can shine like emeralds against the pale, refracted shades of their sandy setting. At times a river which has been repeatedly tapped dries up before it reaches the sea. Then the coast appears deserted and lifeless, like a landscape on the moon, though wonderful in its colours alongside the deep-blue of the sea.

CHRONOLOGICAL TABLES

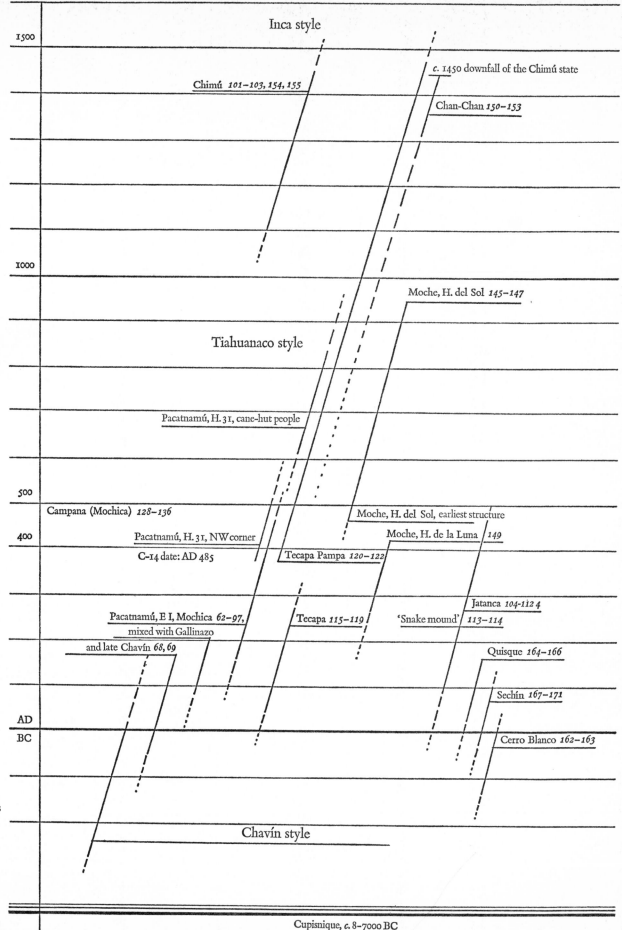

CHRONO-
LOGICAL
TABLES OF
THE SITES
EXCAVATED

NORTH
COAST

Inca style

1500

c. 1450 downfall of the Chimú state

Chimú *101–103, 154, 155*

Chan-Chan *150–153*

1000

Moche, H. del Sol *145–147*

Tiahuanaco style

Pacatnamú, H. 31, cane-hut people

500

Campana (Mochica) *128–136*

Moche, H. del Sol, earliest structure

400

Pacatnamú, H. 31, NW corner

Moche, H. de la Luna | *149*

C-14 date: AD 485

Tecapa Pampa *120–122*

Jatanca *104-112 4*

Pacatnamú, E I, Mochica *62–97,*
mixed with Gallinazo

Tecapa *115–119*

'Snake mound' *113–114*

and late Chavín *68, 69*

Quisque *164–166*

The horizontal
lines under the
names indicate
their approximate
chronological
position.

Sechín *167–171*

AD
BC

Cerro Blanco *162–163*

The oblique lines
stemming from
the horizontal ones
show roughly the
time span of the
appropriate styles
or cultures.

Chavín style

The numbers
following the
entries refer to the
plates.

Cupisnique, *c.* 8–7000 BC
artefacts of palaeolithic character, *123–127*

SOUTH
COAST
AND
SOUTHERN
ANDES

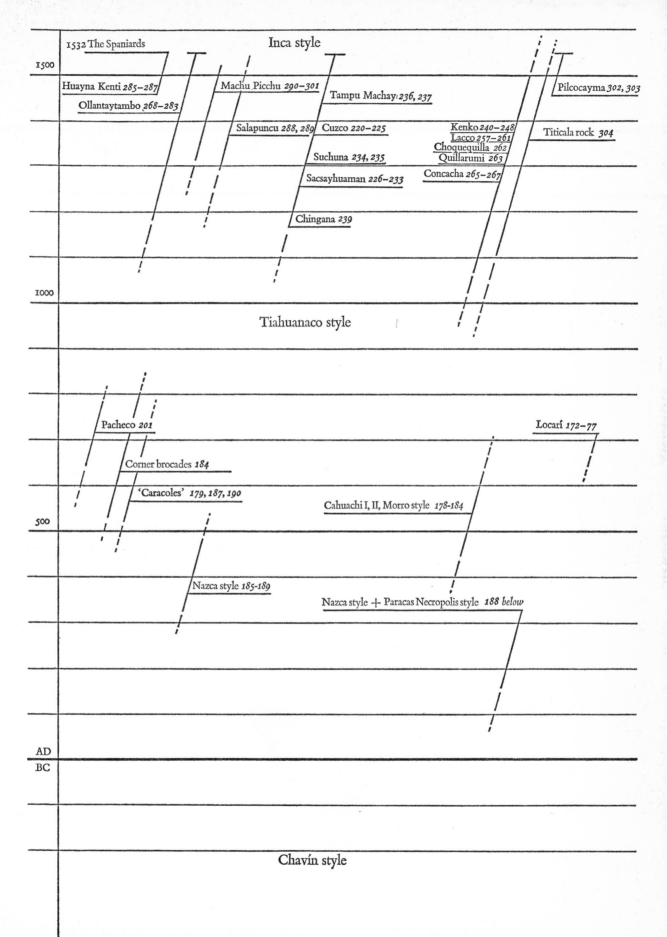

1500

1532 The Spaniards

Inca style

Huayna Kenti *285–287*
Ollantaytambo *268–283*

Machu Picchu *290–301*

Tampu Machay *236, 237*

Pilcocayma *302, 303*

Salapuncu *288, 289* Cuzco *220–225*

Kenko *240–248*
Lacco *257–261*
Choquequilla *262*
Quillarumi *263*

Titicala rock *304*

Suchuna *234, 235*

Sacsayhuaman *226–233*

Concacha *265–267*

Chingana *239*

1000

Tiahuanaco style

Pacheco *201*

Locarí *172–77*

Corner brocades *184*

'Caracoles' *179, 187, 190*

Cahuachi I, II, Morro style *178–184*

500

Nazca style *185-189*

Nazca style + Paracas Necropolis style *188 below*

AD
BC

Chavín style

NOTES ON THE PLATES

It is a pleasing and refreshing experience to fly along the Peruvian coast, above the snow-covered peaks scattered like marble patches amid the dark mass of the Cordilleras, and above a coast of pastel shades, as in a painting by Corot, garlanded with spray from the ceaseless surf of the Pacific Ocean. The line of surf and spray is carried by the Humboldt current and by the steady south-east wind which blows along the coast.

33 *Offshore lie islands* which, like the coastlands, look as though they were dusted with delicate colours. The sea around the islands is deep blue, at times jade green near the coasts, and in winter often covered with sea-mist. Cloud cover can be thick over long stretches of the coast in the winter months. Millions of seabirds live on many of the islands, sustained by the wealth of fish life which flourishes in the cool waters of the Humboldt current.

34 A large *herd of sea-lions* on the flat rocks near Pocusana, south of Lima. They were formerly characteristic of the rocky coastal stretches, where the sea surges over the boulders and washes the flat surfaces. Sea-lions are large, heavy animals, clumsy out of the water, when they hobble along with the aid of their flippers.

I should not expect to find such a herd near Pocusana today – the photograph was taken in 1931. Pocusana has since become the most famous resort south of the capital, and sea-lions do not like human company. In 1931 the cry of the sea-lion could still be heard at night below the high Malecón coast road at Miraflores, a suburb of Lima. In 1938 there were still some sea-lions on the north coast, off the Barranca de Pacatnamú, though their numbers were never comparable with those of the herd illustrated here. In times past these animals must have been at home on many parts of the coast, and will have been well known to the inhabitants of the coastlands.

35 *Condors over Pacatnamú*, a sight which has also become rare nowadays. These massive birds with their huge wing-span were frequent visitors during our 1938 excavations at Pacatnamú. They would come in the morning from the north, male and female together, and gliding on the warm currents which rise from the cliff edge of the plateau, they would hover for minutes on end without sound or movement of the wings, their pinion feathers extended like out-stretched fingers to catch every movement of the air. They would circle above the ruined city, apparently more inquisitive than timid. From time to time they would thrust downwards in a frenzy, just because a tripod was being set up. In the morning they would sit on the edge of the scarp like heraldic figures, with half-open wings, warming themselves in the sun.

A flight over the coast of Peru is not only enjoyable, it also reveals the whole character of the country, the essential features of the environment which have conditioned human culture for thousands of years. Between the green valleys, whose appearance as one flies along is like the recurring theme of a great symphony, stretch desert plains – potential arable land for the future – and *barren* 36 *rocky mountains,* with sand like yellow water solidified in the gorges between. Then another valley oasis draws near, the *Casma valley,* with granite outcrops between the vege- 37 tation of the valley bottom. The Casma valley, like the neighbouring Nepeña valley, is rich in ancient monuments from the time of the Chavín culture (see chart on pp. 16, 17). In this valley lies the temple of Sechín with its row of monoliths carved with remarkable reliefs *(167–171)*. Attribution of the temple to the Chavín culture, however, does not seem to me proven, based as it is on certain elements from pottery decoration, which may permit an estimate of date but give little evidence about the reliefs themselves.

Crescent-shaped dunes are a striking feature of the coastal deserts *(pampas),* slowly moving from south-east to north-west driven by the prevailing south or south-east winds. The wind has modelled the landscape, smoothing or penetrating the rocks in its path with blown sand. Ancient *adobe* (mud-brick) buildings, too, are altered, and the corners and edges of walls and pyramids are rounded off and the spaces between them filled with sand. The shifting dunes *(médanos)* move great distances, encroaching on the

old ruined cities like slinking beasts (104-106). The most
39 splendid shifting dune is the *El Purpur dune* in the Virú
valley, which glistens as one flies above it. The black line
along the left in the photograph is part of the Pan American Highway from Alaska to Chile. The dune is moving
towards the north-east, the bottom left-hand corner of the
photograph. Although no other dune on the north coast is
over a hundred yards wide or thirty feet high, El Purpur is
an enormous formation sixty feet in height; its 'horns'
stretching before it are about half a mile apart (Kinzl, 1958,
pp. 10, 11).

The total length of the dune from tip to tip is over a mile
and a half. Nevertheless, especially when it is seen from the
ground, this bright mountain seems light and airy, as
though hovering. With its surface moulded by the wind
into an interlacing arabesque-like pattern, the dune is like
a work of sculpture. The dune appears to be no longer
moving and it has therefore been supposed that in the
course of time it will slowly break up. Kinzl has doubted
this, since the addition of new sand has not ceased.

It is said that a great *huaca* – a temple or sanctuary – lies
buried under the dune and prevents its movement; thus
the dune is also called simply 'Huaca Purpur'. It would
have to be a very large and high structure to force this
mountain of sand to a halt. The dunes which moved across
the ruined city of Jatanca (104-105) were obviously not
hindered by the very stable *tapia* (cast mud-brick) walls.

In the last decades many valuable antiquities have been
found on and around the El Purpur dune: excellent pottery
in the Mochica style and gold ornaments, some inlaid with
semi-precious stones. Perhaps the name *huaca* originally
signified a cemetery (as it often does) near the dune, which
is now being exploited.

38 This photograph was taken while flying over a *valley in the
southern coastlands*. It is especially narrow, but very vividly
illustrates a typical Peruvian coastal valley. Flying south,
we look downstream towards the sea along a ribbon of
green below the dazzling brilliance of the desert plateau;
it grows narrower as it runs towards the sea, so that it has
almost disappeared near the top edge of the photograph.
Water for the irrigation channels has been drawn continuously from the river until it holds scarcely more than
enough to support a few undemanding thorn-bushes and
huarango trees. Many of the coastal valleys are wider than
this one, yet it epitomizes the features found in the larger
ones: the meandering river on a clear gravel bed, the river
forest, or *monte*, the orderly cultivation and, at the edge of
the green valley bottom, the irrigation canals or *acequias*,

bordered by bushes and trees like a row of dark beads. In
such valleys the oldest cultures of the coastlands grew up
over two thousand years ago as fishing settlements, followed by little valley states, some of which then combined
into larger units giving rise to the development of those
kingdoms encountered and absorbed by the growing Inca
realm.

Artificial irrigation was the alpha and omega of life in these
valleys. Associated with it went the construction of cultivation terraces, transforming the mountainous terrain on the
sloping valley sides to increase the land available for crops.
An impressive example is shown in the *cultivation terraces* 40
of the Rimac valley, in the central coastlands, which are
monumental in character. These terraces are supported by
huge walls of undressed stone which have withstood the
ravages of time. Cultivation terraces are found on the
coast and in the mountains up to heights of over nine
thousand feet. They are a characteristic feature of the
mountain landscape over a wide area. Water was often
brought to the terraced fields from a distance – Garcilasso
tells of aqueducts two hundred miles long and nine to
twelve feet wide – though the fields they served were small.
One of the most famous irrigation canals on the north
coast is the *acequia de Ascope* in the Chicama valley, appa- 41
rently of the pre-Inca, Chimú or Mochica, era. It is carried
on a strong embankment which is particularly impressive
when seen from the air.

An old *canal system* on the west side of the wide *Guadalupe* 42
valley (north of Pacasmayo) is by contrast little known. An ▲
irrigation channel (called today an *acequia madre* or 'mother'
canal) brings water from the Jequetepeque river to the
Charcape hills which lie between the Guadalupe valley
and the sea.

Over a long distance the valley side of the canal had to be
built up, with the uphill edge hewn out of the cliff. The
retaining wall is 5 ft. 6 in. high and almost 3 ft. thick. The
canal is 5 ft. wide at the bottom and 6 ft. 6 in. wide at the
top. It cut through the outer Charcape hills to carry water
to a valley bowl, which today is entirely desert. The rest
of the canal must have been *carved out of the living rock,* 42
which is a yellowish-grey granite. This section of the canal ▼
is some 8 ft. deep, 4 ft. wide at the bottom and 8 ft. wide at
the top. Nowadays it disappears in the valley bottom,
which is scattered with the ruins of various adobe buildings: sacred terraces of tiny dimensions, similar in plan to
those built at Pacatnamú.

The final distribution of the water to the fields was
through *shallow ditches*, laid out almost like a labyrinth. 43

When the water entered the ditches its flow was checked as it passed between the interconnected channels, so that the planted fields were irrigated uniformly. The irrigation system near the desert city of Tecapa *(115, 116)* and the feeder-canal described above *(42, above and below)* are evidence of the technical abilities of the Chimú.

The Inca highway system has already been described in the introduction. An example in the lower Chicama valley is the *highway near Chiquitoy*: about 10 ft. wide, with adobe side walls now in ruins, this section runs dead straight towards the north. The impression that the road is swallowed up in the distance is especially marked here. The section of the *highway running south* from this same point cuts across a ruined pyramid, which appears as a mound in the left background of the plate. The pyramid is built from lumps of clay and is certainly a thousand years older than the road, since for those who built the pyramid (perhaps Mochica people) the siting of the road without regard for the temple buildings would have been unthinkable, both pointless and a sacrilege. From its overriding of the ancient precincts this relatively modern highway would appear to be a work of the fifteenth century, the century of the Inca. Regardless of the pyramids of the ancient gods, it obeys only the directive under which it was planned and built, which was to connect as directly as possible the centre and periphery of a great empire, so that the will of the ruler and his officials, his couriers and army, could penetrate to every part of his territory with the greatest possible speed, for the preservation of the realm.

Further south the *camino real del Inca* (royal highway of the Inca) crosses the *valley of the Jequetepeque*. All trace of it is lost in the valley itself, but on the surrounding stony plateau it is well preserved and runs straight towards the south. At this point it is about 22 ft. wide. On the far side of the valley the parallel lines of its side walls can be seen rising towards the pass of Chocofán.

The *road follows the natural undulations*, and hillocks are surmounted and never cut through. It is obvious that the demands of wheeled transport did not need to be taken into consideration in planning the Inca highways. Ancient Peru had no vehicles, indeed the wheel was unknown both to the Inca and the entire South American continent before the Conquest.

The *side walls* of this section of the road must, according to the chroniclers, originally have stood higher, consisting of rubble-filled stone walls. The core appears to contain an effective binding material since the walls are remarkably firm. On occasion when they have to be removed to make way for the construction of a modern road this can be done only with the aid of a pick-axe. Inca road builders also knew how to drain, strengthen road surfaces by lines of cobbles, embank roads to a height of about 3 ft. and, finally, to cut the road into a mountain side *(51)*.

Few antiquities are more impressive than the sight of an *Inca road crossing the desert, here in the Pampa de Zaña* in northern Peru. No other structure leaves so extensive and striking a mark on the landscape. The road, some 20 ft wide, runs across the arid plain between walls of adobe or stone. Our car was quite at home driving along the road for a few kilometres, until it was halted by deposits of sand. The old road looked like an autobahn which had been buried by sandstorms.

It must not be forgotten that these roads have withstood four hundred years of sandstorms, the sun's intense heat, with dew by night and the damp mists, as well as a conqueror's destruction. Where they have not been submerged by sand or alluvial deposits or swept away by streams, it is still possible to drive on many of them, both on the coast and in the mountains, although they were never intended for wheeled transport. I have been told by engineers that they not infrequently lay motor roads on surviving Inca roads. In the southern Andes near Cuzco sections of the mountain road have been in use since the conquest of 1532, and are still in use today *(208–211)*.

Crossing the Pampa de Zaña one finds sand-covered remains of buildings which may be interpreted as the *rest-houses of Inca times*; these were sited at intervals of twelve to twenty miles for the accommodation of travellers (see pp. *12, 13*).

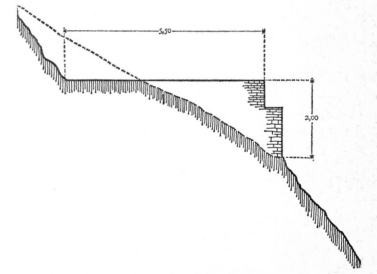

Fig. 1. An Inca road partly cut into the mountain side and partly embanked (see pl. *51*).

50 Aerial view of a typical stretch of highway near Chan-Chan, the ancient capital of the Chimú: the Inca road is crossed by the footings of the Pan American highway (under construction in 1938). Running diagonally across the photograph two of the struts of the aircraft can be seen.

Before leaving the coast road we must draw attention to yet another technical achievement of Inca engineers, *51* namely the laying of a *road along the line of a slope* by cutting into the hill on one side and building up the road surface on the other (fig. 1). This construction is illustrated in the Jequetepeque valley, a little to the north of the Chocofán pass. The road here is about 19 ft. wide overall, some 7 ft. 6 in. of it being cut into the steep rocky slope of the barren mountain while the remainder is embanked. The infill is faced by a stepped wall of worked stones some 6 ft. high and 2 ft. 6 in. thick.

PACATNAMÚ

The principal aim of our 1937–39, 1953–54 and 1962–63 *52, 53* expeditions was the excavation of *Pacatnamú, a deserted ruined city* at the mouth of the river Jequetepeque to the *52* north of Pacasmayo. It lies on a *terrace overlooking the sea*, a desert plateau with barren rocky hills behind. Two of its westerly pyramids, which may be fifteen hundred years old, can be seen as weather-beaten mounds at the top right of the plate. The plateau falls away towards the sea in a steep cliff. In the distance the steep shoreline is hidden in spray rising from the breakers. The city lay undisturbed for centuries until it attracted the attention first of treasure-seekers *(huaqueros)* and later of archaeologists.

53 An aerial view of the *ruined city of Pacatnamú*. It consists of over fifty pyramids and terraces with square walled enclosures between. The most extensive is seen on the right, immediately south of the largest pyramid, H. 1 ('H' being a '*huaca*', or holy place). The predominance of pyramids and terraces in the city plan stands out clearly in the photograph. The terraces (with the possible exception of the large terrace H. 31, which we were to excavate later, *56, 57*) have no independent significance but are appendages of individual pyramids. The grouping of several buildings round a sacred site is most clearly seen in the complex H. 1.

To the north of this pyramid (above it in the photograph) lies an open space bounded to the east (right) by a stepped terrace, which I call the 'eastern outworks' of the pyramid. To the south of the pyramid, as its 'southern outworks',

lies one of the square walled enclosures mentioned above. A number of pyramid complexes have these features to the east and south, though some have works to the east, and fewer to the south, only. All the pyramids are similar, both in plan and elevation; they are squat, stepped constructions of adobe. With the exception of two or three which are turned to the west, all the pyramids face north (as do the graves). By contrast, they are of vastly different dimensions. Some pyramids are 200 ft. wide and over 40 ft. high, others scarcely 16 ft. wide and 6 to 10 ft. high. This similarity in lay-out, combined with big differences in size, leads us to conclude that almost all the pyramids at Pacatnamú belonged to the same cult but that they were erected by groups with greatly differing capacities. A powerful tribe or royal clan would build an imposing pyramid, a small fishing village a modest one. The cult to which the city was dedicated is a matter of conjecture. From the general correspondence in the orientation of pyramids and graves towards the north, we may surmise that it was a cult of the dead which brought different communities from the coastlands and the mountains of northern Peru to erect temple buildings near the sea, according to a set plan. Pacatnamú would then be a religious centre to which people came from all directions.

Not all the pyramids at Pacatnamú are equally old. This can be inferred from the different types of brick used – rectangular flat bricks or of plano-convex section – and their position in the structure. At times both are found in a single structure, as in the case of H. 31 where the plano-convex bricks are in the higher and later layers *(98, right background)*.

As a starting point for dating the pyramids the Institute of Physics of Heidelberg University took C-14 readings from charcoal samples from the north-west corner of terrace H. 31. Readings from three different samples, each taken over a square yard from a deep layer, gave a date AD 485 (with a possible margin of error of 50–100 years on either side). On the evidence of pottery styles found (in 1937–38) in graves in the northern precincts of H. 31 (which also had graves inside and perhaps served as a temple of the dead) this terrace may be ascribed to a period when Mochica and Gallinazo pottery was used concurrently as grave offerings.

The typical aspect of the smaller pyramids is shown by the *Pacatnamú pyramid H. 2* (which lies to the north-east of *54* H. 1). The ramp rises obliquely from the left, and the ▲ terminal wall of the pyramid is clear, crossing the southern edge of the upper platform.

54 The *largest structure at Pacatnamú, pyramid H. 1,* shows the same form as H. 2 but on a far larger scale. A broad ramp ascends over two steps and platforms, the upper bounded to east, south and west by a wall, leaving only the north, the sacred direction, open. A pillared hall was built on the flat ground up to the western base of the terrace H. 31, though still associated with the pyramid; a line of pillar bases is still discernible on the following plate (55) to the left, near the pyramid.

55 This *aerial view of the temple complex H. 1,* taken from the south-east, shows the pyramid as the nucleus of the group. It measures 210 ft. from east to west, 220 ft. from north to south; the prominent ramp is 40 ft. long, and its present height 45 ft., probably somewhat reduced by weathering. Below it to the left in the photograph (that is, behind the pyramid) lie the wide, rectangular southern outworks, with numerous ruined walls and a small pyramid immediately adjacent to the side wall of the large one. Above to the right, and north of H. 1, is an open space, with two very low elongated rectangles as altars. On the eastern side of this space lies a flat, stepped terrace (partly cut off in the plate), the eastern outworks of the pyramid, with a significance for the cult which we have not yet discovered. These are the components of a temple complex at Pacatnamú: the pyramid, the eastern outworks and the southern outworks, with the addition in some temples of a fourth element, an altar on the open space in front (in H. 1 there are two).

In the right foreground the plateau on which the city stands falls away to the Jequetepeque river. The plateau is composed of a gravel conglomerate, which in places is as hard as concrete.

The terrace H. 31 can be seen, near the upper edge of the photograph.

56, 57 *Terrace H. 31 at Pacatnamú* must have had a particular significance, although it was originally only a stepped terrace. Today it is pitted with holes, with a yawning crater in the middle, which suggests that treasure-seekers must have taken a rich haul. Any site which looks as though it had been bombed is the result of their activities, and they themselves speak of 'ploughing' a rich site. Not only was the terrace itself disturbed but the ground to the north of the pyramid is strewn with craters. North was the sacred direction for H. 31 as well, as was confirmed by our later discovery of a northern ramp (98). Similarly the ramps of neighbouring pyramids, H. 13 (upper left corner) and H. 12, lie like pointers to the north. Despite the disturbances we decided to excavate on and in front of

terrace H. 31, though we had not anticipated the good stone walls which emerged from the débris. The base of the north-west corner of the temple-terrace is shown in pl. 56.

Our aim of discovering the exact position of the four corners beneath the rubble shown in pl. 57 succeeded beyond expectation, giving the dimensions: north side 180 ft., south side 177–180 ft., west side 215 ft., east side 212–215 ft. The apparent height of 10 to 13 ft. proved in fact to be 16 to 20 ft. when the footings were excavated. The other corners were not as well preserved as the north-western one.

The walls were sloping, which suggests a Mochica construction. The terrace may be ascribed to a culture in which Mochica and Gallinazo coexisted without merging, as already suggested in the note (q.v.) on pl. 53. There is confirmation from the C-14 readings from three charcoal samples from the foot of the west wall near the north-west corner.

At a distance of 4 ft. 6 in. from the foot of the north face a 3-ft. high vertical wall of adobe was found (see pl. 56) which ran to the north-east corner parallel to the north side, interrupted only by the ramp. The purpose of this feature is not known. It can only be said that it must be later than the inclined terrace wall. The narrow passage between the two was filled with clay rubble, with sherds and traces of burnt material in places. The débris was high enough to obscure most of the terrace wall. It must betoken conflict around H. 31, in which the temple-terrace was destroyed. The clearest evidence of destruction by combat and fire is found in numerous fragments of clay, fluted in the manner of Greek pillars. These are the remnants of the clay daub, often baked hard and brick-red, from the inner and outer walls of reed huts. The impression of the reeds (about an inch thick) and of the twine which held them together was preserved in the clay when it was burnt, and this alone has survived. An identical phenomenon was observed by Sir Leonard Woolley at Ur of the Chaldees in Mesopotamia.

The assumption that the reed huts at Pacatnamú were painted is not unsupported. I have found wall painting on similar huts near a small temple complex at Licapa and on a cella of clay tiles on the pyramid of Fachén, both in the Chicama valley. At Fachén typical Mochica whirls were rendered in many-coloured variations, while Licapa included a large coloured eye (similar to that illustrated in pl. 100) which our excavators immediately named 'the sun'.

The people who built the reed huts must have lived after AD 500. The results of our excavations make it probable that they belonged to the final phases of a Mochica-Gallinazo culture; the destruction of the H. 31 terrace ended an epoch. In the centuries before AD 500 these two styles are found side by side at Pacatnamú, where Mochica textiles occur in their purest form. The pottery from the chamber graves, of which we excavated three (E I, M XI and M XII), however, shows that Gallinazo ware usually predominated, even when Mochica jars were present in their classic form (like the painted ware in fig. 6). The impression is of a small but significant Mochica intrusion among a Gallinazo population.

This would signify that the Mochica vessels and textiles were brought for burial from elsewhere. It would then seem more likely that the H. 31 terrace was constructed by a Gallinazo architect, a conclusion supported by its size and the variety of its brick forms, which at the type site of Huaca Gallinazo in the Virú valley Wendell Bennett has designated as typical of Gallinazo II.

Supporting the assumption that Mochica folk were present among the people of the reed huts is a remarkable 58, 59 fragment of a *modelled head-vase,* found in the débris between the sloping base of H. 31 and the wall running parallel to its north side. When it was found the title 'king of Assyria' immediately occurred both to myself and to a Peruvian colleague. The title is suggested primarily by the bead-like pendants hanging from the temples, apparently representing ornaments or insignia of turquoise. The effect is heightened by embossed discs in front of the ears, probably copying a gold original.

These are surmounted by a double, indented crown. And lastly there are two short tufts of moustache springing from the corners of the mouth. Heads with similar bead pendants, and with beaded brow fillets, are not infrequent in the north coastal region. They represent important people, but not individuals. What is portrayed is not a particular king or priest, but the contemporary notion of the regal or priestly. The institution of kingship and priesthood, with its magical significance, would properly be entreated in these sculptural portrayals. Heads like that illustrated in pls 58 and 59 are reminiscent of the plastic art of high Mochica culture and may be termed stylistically 'late Mochica'.

A peculiar detail of the head is the moustache, or rather, what appears to be a moustache. It springs abruptly from the corners of the mouth and would seem to be artificial, as was the dress beard of an Egyptian pharaoh. There are numerous modelled heads in the Mochica culture which are, as it were, accoutred with these tufts of moustache. Almost invariably they start near the corners of the mouth, and individual hairs are never depicted. Indigenous South Americans do not have facial hair, so that this feature is surprising, and suggests that it may have had some special significance for the Mochica people which is not known to us.

A *fragment of a head from Pacatnamú H. 8* (upper layers) 60 showing the ceremonial moustache somewhat obliterated by weathering and attrition and here lying nearer the centre of the upper lip. The temple pendants are not beaded but clearly represent the same part of the insignia as the beaded pendants of the previous head. The modelling is also similar, although firmer in the eyes and mouth, which are nonetheless expressive. Round the chin there is what appears to be white kerchief over applied clay, represented by irregular strokes of whitewash. Like the previous example this fragment may be assigned to the sixth or seventh century AD.

A *carved wooden head from Pacatnamú H. 12* in a quite 61 different tradition. What this model lacks in technique is made up by its expressiveness. The primitive approach and handling of the eyes are consistent with Gallinazo work of the first or second century AD, though this date must rank as an informed guess.

View of the *opened burial chamber of grave E I* in front of 62 the *Pacatnamú terrace H. 31.* For excavation the terrace forecourt was gridded along the points of the compass. By excavating systematically we soon disclosed several superimposed layers of clay which covered the graves. The graves lay below at three levels, 5 ft., 6 ft. 6 in. and 13 ft. At the 5 ft. level the bodies were wrapped in shrouds; at the two lower levels cane coffins were used. In the M XII grave (at 6 ft. 6 in.) only the impression made by the cane coffins was visible, the coffins having been reduced by the damp sand which had been used to fill the chamber before it was sealed. By contrast the coffins were free of sand in the chamber grave E I (fig. 2). The discovery in 1938 of this undisturbed shaft and chamber grave was exciting. The domed clay seal was first visible, with a depression indicating the position of the grave on its floor. Above were indications of three postholes. Further excavation revealed adobe bricks which had been held in position by the posts. To the left was a wall of adobe, curving forward, and to the right this wall ran in an east-west direction along the hard gravel. The curved section proved to be the entrance to the grave.

Since the wall began to project forward as it continued upwards it could not immediately be followed without danger of collapse. Instead the chamber was examined from the top, revealing a low, domed cavity running south in the gravel. Initially it was seen to contain three long cane coffins lying uncovered; the last was unusually wide and had been pushed obliquely into the chamber. There were numerous vases to left and right. The coffins brought to mind Egyptian mummies, especially in the ceremonial binding round the head-piece, with two lengths of regularly twisted twine running up and down the centre of the coffin, interlaced at approximately twelve-inch intervals (64). The wide coffin on the right (62) appeared not to have this ornamental binding. As in the case of the remains found in the graves at the second level it had a simple type of binding.

The burials were covered with canvas while the ground above and around the vault was cleared (a wearying task not popular with the workmen). The terminal wall, supported by nine posts of huarango wood, was rather irregular. The lower adobe bricks had been pushed out of place and the upper ones were set obliquely like sealing slabs. It must be assumed that the wall was broken through and replaced more than once during later burials. The superimposition of the coffins speaks for a series of burials. Recovery of the grave contents began with the pottery. Only a few pieces were outstanding, such as a black graphite flask (68, 69) with a remarkable relief of snakes encircling a god, and a little owl with inset mother-of-pearl eyes (66). Both vessels belong with the lower and older coffins; the first was in coffin g and is used to characterize this burial.

Plate-like pumpkin bowls are innumerable, since many have disintegrated into leaf-like pieces. On and around the coffins were the skull and bones of sacrificed llamas (65). Discs of plaited rushes were found placed, perhaps ceremonially, on three of the coffins. They are like thin basket covers, but their significance is unknown.

It became apparent that there were three upper coffins, which we designated a, b, and c (from right to left in pl. 62); a was covering coffin d, with b and c above coffin e. In all there were nine cane coffins in the vault, each with a single burial. In addition we found the remains of three uncovered skeletons, intermingled, immediately behind the post wall; since they are unlikely to be later burials, we take them to be human sacrifices associated with the coffin a.

At a depth of 13 ft. the chamber grave E I was tunnelled sideways into the conglomerate from the bottom of a short shaft. The other chamber graves, M XI and M XII, at this level were similarly constructed. But while E I and M XII were undisturbed, M XI had been broken into by treasure-seekers, an occurrence which can be dated by a Spanish oil jug left on the site; it was of a type imported from Estremadura in the sixteenth or seventeenth century. Coffin a (on the right in pl. 62) contained the peerless tapestries shown in pls 71–73. Its lower right corner had been broken off, apparently because it was too large for the vault and was damaged when the wall was put back. Woven fragments (74), and especially embroidery, were found in the narrower coffin b (alongside). Coffin c was on the left (89–90), covered with pottery.

The lowest coffins were very decomposed and we had great difficulty in lifting them. The bindings would

Fig. 2. Section through the shaft-grave E I at Pacatnamú.

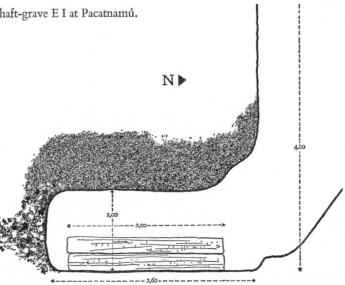

N ▶

scarcely withstand being cleaned with a soft paint-brush, and broke even when the coffins were lifted with the greatest care. Yet it was impossible to open the coffins *in situ* since the chamber was too cramped and encumbered with the other deposits. Even photographic record was impossible, not only because of the dim light, but on account of the continuous dusty wind which threatened to damage the camera mechanism with particles of blown sand.

From the sand and débris filling the shaft of chamber grave

63 E I came a *fragment of a clay head,* with the stern features of a watchman at the tomb. The treatment of the nose is interesting and resembles that on a small copper mask from one of the oldest E I burials, *d (80).*

64 The careful *binding on the cane coffins* in chamber grave E I; also shown are the evenly twisted pieces of twine which run the length of the coffin. Between the coffins is a jar with an animal relief on the shoulder.

65 The unique *ceremonial binding of the head of a cane coffin* can be seen in the photograph. Among the numerous grave offerings are pottery, pumpkin bowls with remains of food (fish, probably fifteen hundred years old), llama bones and a woven rush disc which we do not consider to be a cover since the bowl which can be seen in the middle of the photograph was uncovered when the chamber was opened.

A small pottery vessel (without a stirrup spout) in the shape

66 of an *owl with inlaid shell eyes.* It belongs with the earliest burials from the bottom layer of the grave. Incrustation is, however, a technique not usually found in examples of Mochica work.

67 A second *owl characteristically early Mochica*; an outstanding piece, modelled with confidence, and with a ring spout deriving from an earlier, Chavín-directed period. It comes from the 6 ft. 6 in. layer, where the burials were not in chamber graves but were deposited in hollows excavated in the rock surface ('tub-graves'). Though the cane coffins are the same as in the lowest layer, the canes and their bindings are much more decayed and have at times disappeared. Grave offerings at the two layers are however so closely related that one may speak of the same culture. One may surmise that those buried in these grave hollows belonged to the entourage of the dead in the chamber graves.

It was the discovery of this owl from one of the undisturbed graves at the 6 ft. 6 in. level (A VIII) in 1937–38 which determined us to excavate the ground in front of terrace H. 31 completely.

With this *black graphite jar* we go back to an older style, *68, 69* the Chavín horizon style. At this site it is still contemporary with the Mochica, although the expressively archaic style does not appear in its full glory. We find its final effects mixing with Mochica and Gallinazo work. The most brilliant Chavín period had been in the centuries before Christ. Reliefs on stone stele at the type site, Chavín de Huantar, show a similar stylization. Also reminiscent of the Chavín style is the white infilling in the excised pattern of our jar. The base is decorated in the same way *(69, below).* I have seen the same lime-white colouring an a wall relief, depicting fishes in the coastal Chavín style, at Cerro Sorcape in the Chicama valley.

Thus among the pottery in the chamber grave E I at least three styles are represented, which at other sites appear successively: Mochica, Gallinazo and a brand of Chavín. This presents difficulties. Even allowing for a series of burials, the nine coffins in the grave can cover at most a hundred years. The succession of three important styles in a single grave cannot be compressed into a century. In addition, the Mochica style would then have to be fixed too early. One can assume that not all this very various pottery originated at Pacatnamú itself. The pyramid city must have been a place of pilgrimage and people would come from great distances, either for cult celebrations or to bury a prominent person. The pilgrims would bring their own pottery and offerings with them.

If we were asked to pick out from among the E I finds the pottery most likely to represent the product of the local coastal industry round Pacatnamú it would be that in the so-called Gallinazo style which, as becomes ever more apparent, was the early style of the coastal area. It accounts for the mass of the finds, with Mochica and occasional Chavín-like elements brought in from outside, perhaps from a distance. Characteristic of the Gallinazo style are the simple forms, with decorative features merely indicated by pinching up and impressing the clay (fig. 3, centre and right), with incised and punched ornament and with negative painting. This last trait was not encountered in our 1937–38 excavations. W. Duncan Strong noticed the problem, describing the E I find as 'strongly suggesting the Gallinazo style, save that no negative painting was noted' (1952, p. 232 and 241). However in our 1953–54 campaign negative painting was found on site H. 14 at Pacatnamú, not far from H. 31. We also found negative painting in the ruined city of Jatanca twelve miles southeast of Pacatnamú, in the Paiján desert south of San Pedro de Lloc.

The black graphite *jar with white infill, depicting snakes encircling a god (68, 69)*, could have come from an area where Chavinoid stylistic elements, and beliefs, persisted into the third or fourth century AD. W. Duncan Strong has suggested (loc. cit., p. 232) the region of Kuntur Wasi, a Chavín centre in the mountains east of Pacatnamú. The Mochica element in grave E I is emphasized by the textiles – slit (or 'kelim') tapestry *(71–73)* and embroidery *(74, 78, 79)* – which were found in unexpected profusion in coffins *a*, *b*, *c* and *g*; and by tattooing on the forearm and hand of a woman buried in coffin *b*. Scarcely any weaving which could certainly be described as Mochica work was known until the discovery of grave E I in 1938.

with spiral relief on the shoulder of its squat body. It is very similar to that associated with burial *c* in chamber grave M XII *(95)*. The spiral whirl is a typical symbol of the Mochica style, alike on pottery (almost like a coat-of-arms on the breast of the fighting warriors or gods from grave M XI) and in wall painting on a cella in the Fachén pyramid in the Chicama valley. With it the dead man was identified as an important individual (to judge from his equipment) in a Mochica cultural community. In this instance the vessel has an almost hieroglyphic significance, although we cannot now understand which society it refers to and where it existed, since the original names of the Mochica are unknown to us.

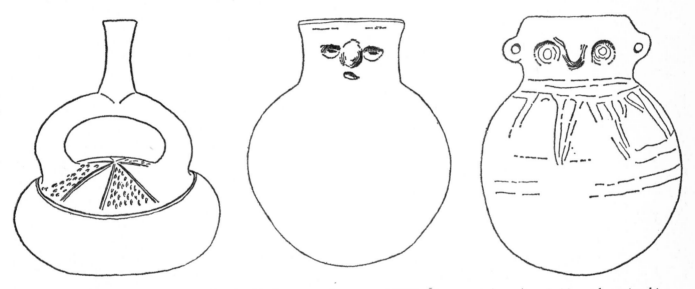

Fig. 3. (Left) Pottery flask with incised and stabbed ornament from grave M XII at Pacatnamú; (centre) a primitive and unpainted jar from grave M XII; (right) pottery jar lightly washed with white, from grave E I at Pacatnamú.

In 1930 A. L. Kroeber had written, 'No weaving is known which can certainly be ascribed to the early Chimú era (Mochica) . . . Uhle found none in his series of more than thirty graves near Moche. Even a small collection of woven fragments from an undoubted early Chimú context would accordingly be of historical significance'. In 1946 W. Duncan Strong found fragments of weaving in a Mochica grave in the Huaca de la Cruz in the Virú valley (loc. cit., pl. XXIX). The Mochica weaving from Pacatnamú has not withstood fifteen hundred years without damage. What is left is nevertheless so considerable that important new iconographic as well as technical knowledge may be expected from its study.

70, 71 The *opening of coffin a in the chamber grave E I at Pacatnamú.* The first thing encountered when the covering canes were removed was a grey-black jar with a stirrup handle and

The corpse was laid with the head to the south and feet to the north, wrapped in shrouds which at first did not excite particular interest. The head was covered with a layer of white, unspun cotton. The importance of the dead man in his society was indicated by the remains of a blue feather cloak which could be seen glinting in several places. To the right lay a llama vertebra, the burial sacrifice of an animal from the mountains.

The *white cotton shroud was carefully lifted* to reveal *(71)* the world of the gods depicted in a tapestry which lay folded over the head. It was as though the dead man were singing the ancient songs of the gods in an ethereal voice for the living he had left behind; for all men would know the words which went with these pictures, and they could therefore represent the sacred charms which would influence the fate of man.

The photograph in pl. *71* was taken looking down at the top of the skull to show the little fox-god, holding a giant rattle in his raised hand like a banner before him. Laid across the 'codex' cloth and over the face of the skull is a cord of fine, dark-yellow cotton twine, doubtless of significance since it was also used to bind the head and hands of the burial in coffin *b (75–77)*. Fragments were also found round the hands and feet of the body in this coffin, *a*.

The patterned cloth is not an item of clothing or a cover for the head. It was folded and placed on the head, but held in folds by a few stitches so that it would be impossible to use it as a hat or head scarf. It was not worked for a practical purpose but as a 'text' to accompany the dead person in the world of the gods. Similarly the famous Paracas tapestry in the Göteborg museum, also found folded and on the breast of a mummy, was no article of clothing. Both this, with its border of three-dimensional figures, and the Pacatnamú cloth worked with pictures are clearly in the nature of religious codices, as are many other ancient Peruvian textiles.

73 ▼ The *pictorial cloth* from coffin *a* in grave E I unfolded. Little more that half of the middle section is preserved. Round this section on a light field is a darker, sombre border and beyond this at the lower left corner a further band of a lighter colour, evidently the remains of a border which encircled the whole. In the centre section one can recognize a gabled roof with a border of clubs. The roof timbers terminate in big serpent heads. Little animal demons are flying about over the roof. The scene terminates above with a darker strip, the lower edge scalloped as though to depict clouds. The centre of the strip is filled by a row of leafy plants which look like growing maize. Placed thus in the heavens over the temple roof they could have a symbolic significance since rainfall was essential for the growth of maize, the subsistence crop of ancient Peru.

The interior of the temple shows a scene of the gods, though the principal figure is unfortunately half destroyed. The god is lifting his arm and above his hand hovers a great bird. His head is covered by a helmet or cap from which two long feathers rise up to terminate in serpent heads. As part of his insignia the god wears a remarkable belt, with the ends reaching the ground. Behind him stands the little fox figure *(71)* with his rattle-staff. To the left is the twisting figure of a serpent-headed demon, and below a pair of upright animal-like creatures are holding what is perhaps a shield between them.

Beyond the possible maize-field above and below the temple, there lies at the bottom a dark and sombre section inhabited by ghostly figures which are difficult to distinguish but which must be regarded as belonging with the central scene since they are enclosed within the same border.

The theme of a building with serpent beam terminals and a god (or priest) inside is already known from one of the finest vase paintings in the Mochica style (fig. 4) in the Museum für Völkerkunde, Berlin. Only part of the painting is represented on the Pacatnamú cloth but the similarity to the left-hand portion is obvious. On the other hand, the painting lacks the dark border which contributed to our, admittedly conjectural, interpretation of the central scene on the cloth.

Of the brighter band we have taken to be an outer border of the cloth only the fragment shown on the bottom left is preserved. It is composed of two similar scenes, the left and larger one almost completely preserved. Again the context is a gabled building with serpent-headed beams and a row of clubs on the roof. Inside, however, are two figures in ceremonial dress facing each other, each gripping with one hand a long staff which terminates in the head of a man or a god apparently carved in wood. Junius Bird illustrates a similar group (*Art and Life in Old Peru*, 1962, p. 172 and fig. 23), though here the upper half of the staff is granulated like a huge maize cob, with a head growing out from the top, like a god of maize.

The left-hand figure in the Pacatnamú scene is wearing an animal mask, probably a jaguar mask. A tail hangs down behind him from under a short skirt.

A second serpent-building (which comes up to the bottom right-hand edge of the cloth fragment) is only partly visible. We may almost be bold enough to assume that there was originally a row of these gabled buildings running round the central scene, that is, a certain number of serpent-roofed houses round the large central temple. Since the lay-out is roughly a square, they could have been arranged to conform with the points of the compass. It is not impossible that they stood in some relation to the calendar year, which in ancient Peru – as in Mexico and in the Maya lands – played a decisive role in religious affairs. Sacred wisdom derived from the calendar. It was not just a basis for historical reckoning, but was directed by the gods. All this can be inferred from the religious scenes on textiles in the Tiahuanaco style, the second horizon style, which in many parts of the coast followed the Mochica and its contemporaries further

28

south. And cultural continuity in ancient Peru, already emphasized by Seler, is most evident in religion.

72 A *second pictorial cloth in rich slit tapestry*, a short skirt from around the hips of the body in coffin *a* in grave E I. The

along the lower margin, may have had a similar purpose. Finally, the body in burial *a* was clothed in a mantle, fragmentary remains of which were found on the chest and back. It is illustrated in Doering, 1951 (p. 226, fig. 2).

Fig. 4. Vase painting in the Mochica style from north Peru. Museum für Völkerkunde, Berlin (see pl. *73* and p. 28).

main frieze depicts a row of large sea-shells with anthropomorphic demons lying on their furrowed surfaces, as though they were driving these huge beasts or being carried on their backs. These snake-like shelled creatures have serpent heads, with long antennae like those of a snail. They have large forefeet and their bodies are divided into six or seven sections, each with a central cross. Crosses can betoken eyes, but here appear to represent stars. The border frieze below contains a series of squares in which the shelled creatures appear in miniature (the shells top left) on a light ground, similarly stylized but without the mounted demon or god. There is a hint that this picture world represents the adjuration of water, i. e. a fertility rite in which the sacred calendar would have played a decisive role.

The Brooklyn Museum owns a Mochica skirt, similar to the Pacatnamú example, from Paracas, over 550 miles further south (N. Zimmern, *The Brooklyn Museum*, 1949, no. 19). The pendent strips along its edge are absent in the skirt from Pacatnamú, though the light squares

It can there be seen that the central field was taken up by a large cartouche containing a cross of figures resembling those on the giant shells of the skirt frieze. The continuously recurring cross motif of ancient Peruvian myth and art may denote the stars and their heavenly movements. The pictorial textiles found with the burials are unmistakable evidence of their exclusively Mochica character, and furthermore of the importance of the dead man.

An embroidered cloth from coffin *b*, middle of the three 74 upper burials in grave E I, is again indicative that the dead ▲ person, here a woman, was a Mochica of high rank. The head-veil, embroidered with big bright flowers, lay beneath a turban of yellow twine. The crosses in the middle of the flowers are seen on other Mochica textiles to signify eyes or stars, apparently interchangeably. The partly skeletalized body of the young woman was wrapped in a *loosely* 74 *woven cloth* embroidered with stepped volutes, similar to ▼ the relief decorating the base of the vessel illustrated in pl. *69*.

75 The surprisingly *well-preserved head of the eighteen-year old girl* in coffin *b* (age determination by the anthropologist Professor Mollison). When the covering cotton padding (which was perhaps a protective taboo) was removed, the light-brown face was revealed with a skin like fine old parchment. The black hair was bound round with yellow twine, which was either richer than that in burial *a*, or better preserved, as was the binding on the hands *(76, 77)*.

76, 77 *Decorative tattooing* on the right forearm of the girl in coffin *b* (the left arm had decomposed). The little figures are in pure Mochica style (fig. 5). The back of the hand is also tattooed, and the figures first came to light there when a red layer covering the skin was removed. There are still red patches on the skin in many places, especially on the back of the hand and wrist, painted over the tattooing.

It is interesting that the British Museum guide (p. 46, fig. 42 and p. 44, fig. 41) shows an arm carved from bone with incised small figures resembling those illustrated here in fig. 5, and perhaps representing tattooing. And it is again possible that the figures depicted may have an astrological significance.

The body in coffin *g* of grave E I (one of the lower burials) had an *embroidered cloak of loosely woven cloth*. The decoration embroidered in red and yellow, which are remarkably bright colours for the Mochica palette, included the stylized head of the ray-fish, frequently depicted as a demon in Mochica art. It is closely related to the embroidery on the cloak from coffin *b (74, below),* and the two burials cannot be far separated in time. 78, 79

Plates *78* and *79* show the cloth as it was discovered and after it had been cleaned and restored by Dr. S. Müller-Christensen of Munich, to whom we are indebted for her invaluable help in the conservation of our various textile finds.

Two of the lower coffins, *h* and *d,* contained thin sheets of copper. In coffin *h* four rectangular sheets mounted on a reed backing lay like a shield over the left hand. In coffin *d* a thin *ornamental copper sheet with a little mask* lay over the 80 lower part of the body, but was broken into many pieces. Originally the mask had a copper disc gloriole loosely attached by thin wires, though both had oxidized and fallen away. It strongly recalls little round, handled discs on a fox-head of copper and gold (?) found with three

Fig. 5. Tattooed figures in the Mochica style, on the arm and hand of burial E I *b* at Pacatnamú (pls *76, 77*).

masks in the underground chamber at Huaca de la Luna near Moche, and now in the Linden Museum, Stuttgart. The treatment of the nose on the mask has a close resemblance to that of the fragmentary head which is illustrated in pl. *63*.

These connections serve to fix burial g in the transition from early to full Mochica culture already indicated on stylistic grounds for the E I burials on the evidence of the textiles and tattooing, and they may then be dated to about the third and fourth centuries AD.

continued on p. 81

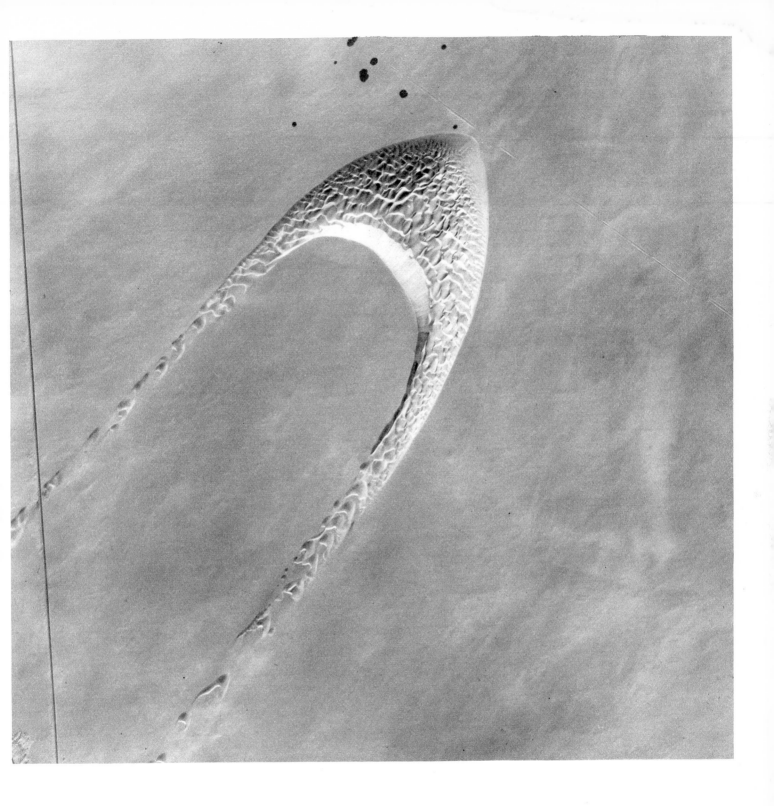

41

51

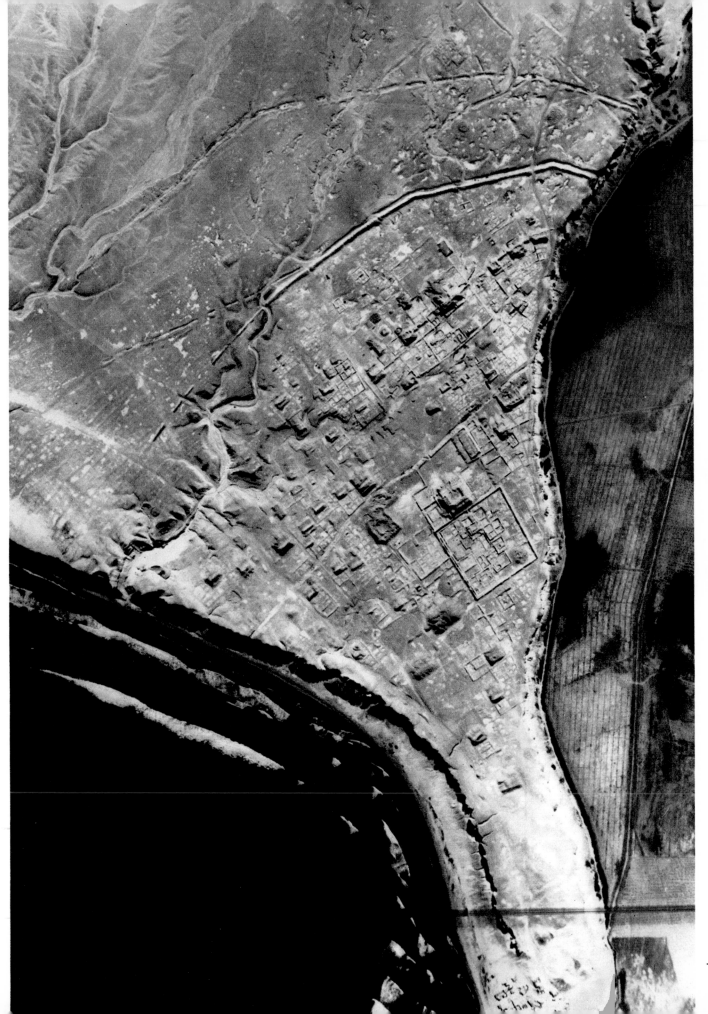

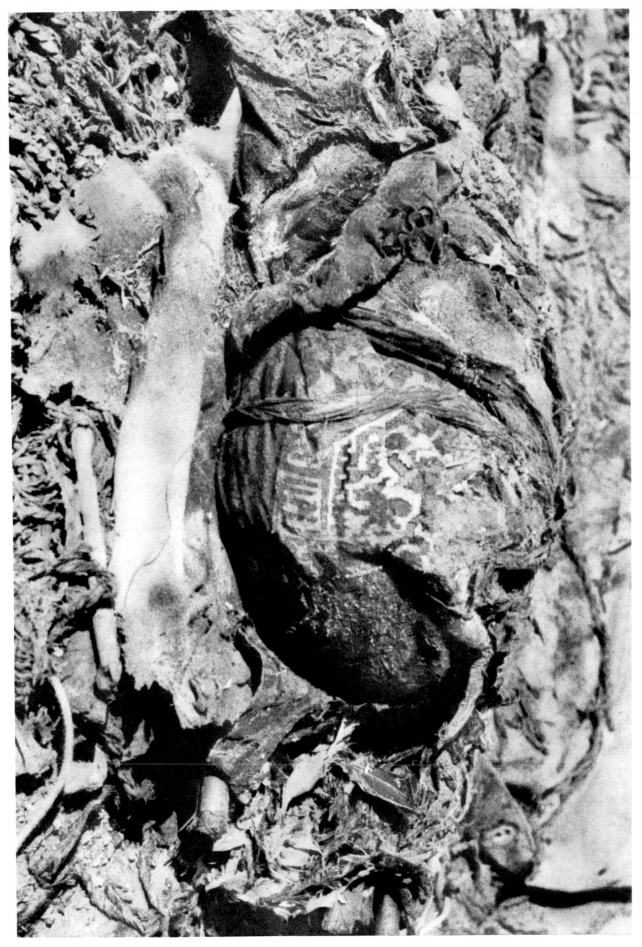

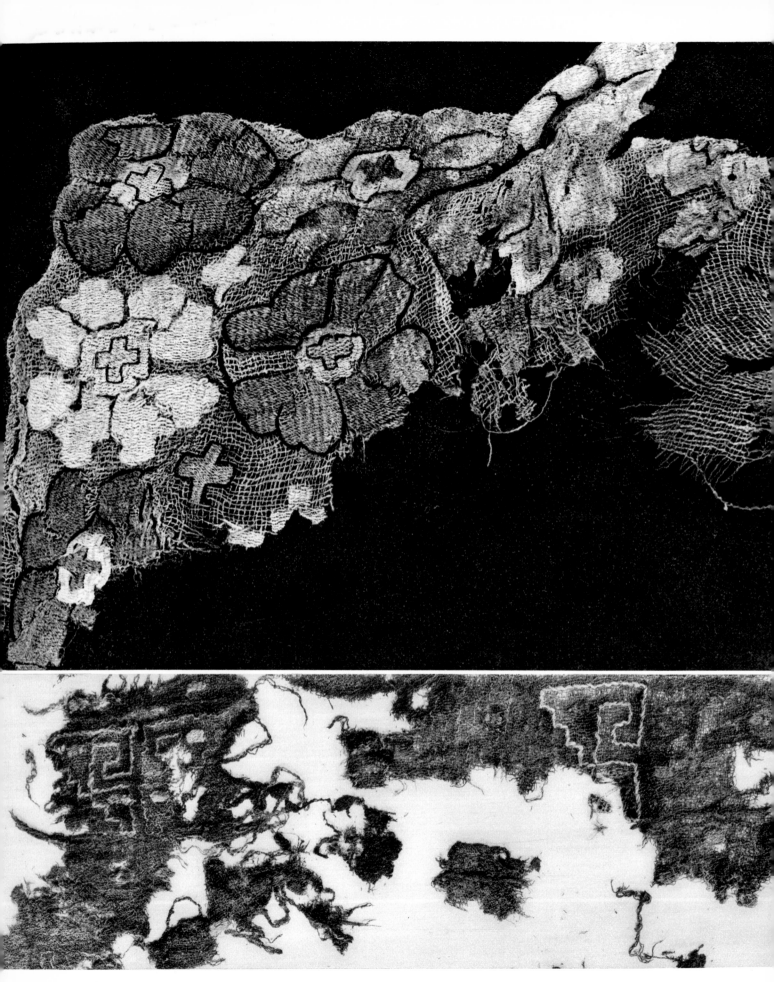

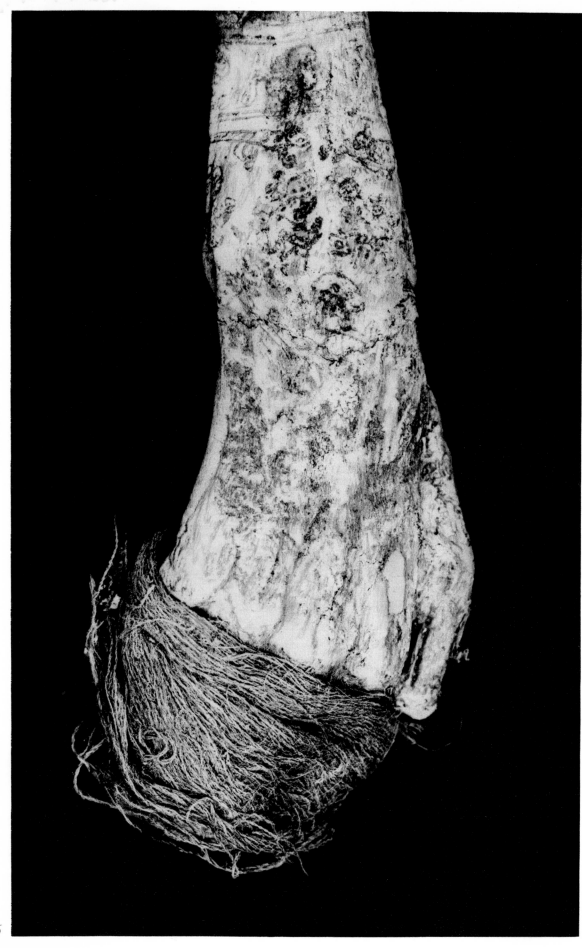

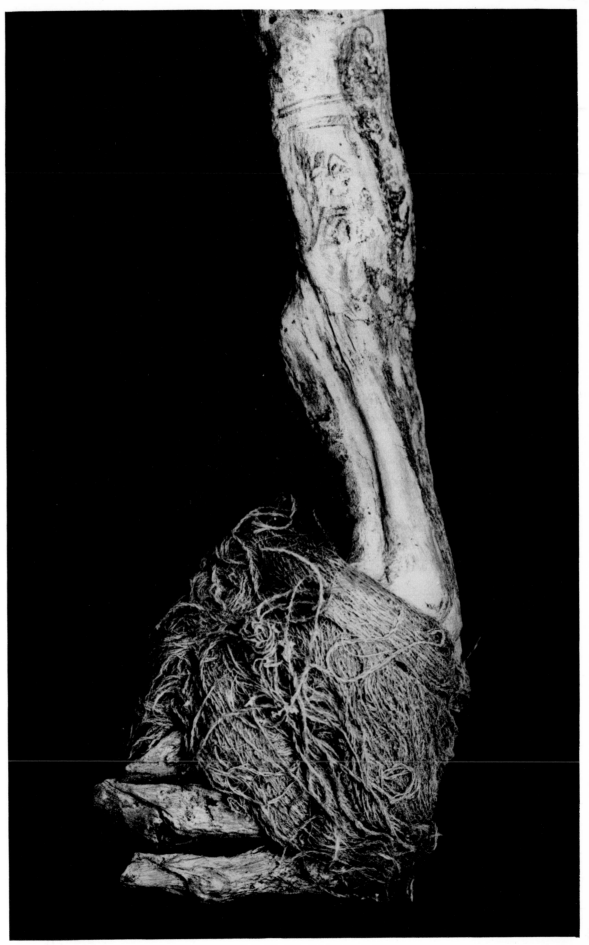

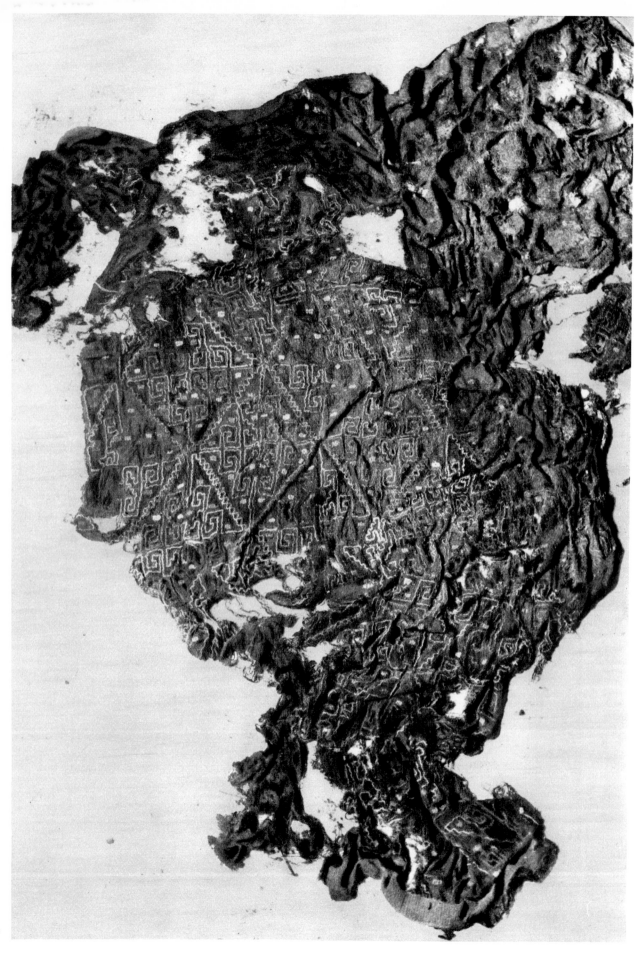

89 *Necklace of carved bone plates with shell inlay* found on the skeleton in the third upper coffin, *c*, in the chamber grave E I at Pacatnamú. The central figure is a frog, being attacked on one side (below) by a bird and on the other (above) by a lizard whose body and tail are represented on the adjacent five plates. The necklace came to light (after lying undisturbed for over fifteen hundred years) when

90 the raw cotton cover was lifted from the *face of the head in coffin c*. The head and foot of the lizard can be seen under the jaw, with the frog nearby. A sheet of copper, oxydized green, lay over the skull's incisors. Copper as a grave offering or amulet is frequent with Pacatnamú burials, e.g. in E I coffin *a* it was found in the mouth, on the hands and on the feet. The richest copper offerings were found with burials in the third chamber grave, M XII. (M XI had been robbed in the sixteenth or seventeenth century and so could not be compared exactly.)

The lay-out of M XII, which was undisturbed, was clear. A rectangular shaft, with the north wall inclining inwards like a steep ramp, opens into a tunnel-like horizontal burial chamber closed by a wall of adobe. In front of this wall on the floor of the shaft in the anteroom of the chamber we found the same assortment of pottery as in E I and M XI. Alongside seven large globular jars, roughly surfaced and with faces partly pinched up on the neck, was a

91 single *Mochica jar in the shape of a mythical beast,* a 'dragon' with spines on its back and tail and rolled volutes on the snout. It is painted in the light-brown typical of the Mochica style. However some older and obviously alien elements are perceptible, not only in the dragon emblem but also in the dark zones between the wavy lines. One gets the impression of the last workings of a coastal Chavín style, in Mochica dress. As pottery associated with the dead in the chamber will show, despite the preponderance of Gallinazo ware, the fashion in M XII was set by the Mochica style.

The 'dragon' lay in a deep infill of sand beside two Gallinazo urns and near a remarkable copper club; a second club was later found to the west on the floor of the shaft, and another beside burial *a* inside the chamber *(93, above)*. Two copper sandals or soles represented an unusual feature; they were stuck obliquely in the sand near some decomposed human leg bones, and must have been placed there only after the shaft had begun to be filled in. These copper sandals, which are quite unsuited for any practical purpose, emphasize the significance of copper in the cult of the dead. Clearly the dead were equipped with copper objects, found in their hands, on their arms, feet and lips and in the mouth.

The body of an unusually large llama was laid over the skeleton as a sacrificial offering. The grave chamber of M XII, a low vault similar to E I cut into the rock, had (like the shaft) been filled with fine blown sand before it was closed. This very much complicated an examination of the burials, especially since the roof was so low that the chamber could be entered only on hands and knees. The skeletons had to be excavated in sections, and the nearer, lower parts cleared and removed before work could start on the upper parts and heads.

While excavating the lower part of the burial *a* skeleton *a black graphite jar* was found deposited with the body. It 92 represents a warrior wearing a ceremonial bird mask beneath his big Mochica helmet. Near the black bird lay a number of copper bells of different sizes which, it appeared, had originally been strung around the wrist of the dead man.

The upper part of the body was then slowly disengaged from the sand and finally the *head wearing a cap-helmet of* 93 *gilded copper discs*, in which individual discs overlapped ▲ like scales. Many of them must have disintegrated, and this would account for the green colouring on the top of the skull. The discs have a perforation in the centre and must have been sewn in place on a cloth cap. Over and behind the head before it was lifted the decayed threads of cotton cloth were visible; while they looked sound, they fell apart at the slightest touch. The metal cap must have come down over the temples since there were still discs there *in situ*.

Somewhat lower and in the region of the ears lay *round* 93 *disc ear-rings:* an outer circlet with applied bead rim round ▼ a central disc with an inlay of small flat turquoise pieces. This ornamentation appears to have been overlaid with gold leaf. The wooden plug which fastened the disc to the lobe was found in the right ear.

Under the cloth wrapping (which fell away almost at once) of the head there were two engraved bone pins. On either side of the head and across the cervical vertebrae the soil was dotted with fine tubular shell beads which must have belonged to a long necklace encircling the throat several times. Three large copper rattles with wedge-shaped handles came to light on the right shoulder and near them a thin copper club, oxydized green, which must clearly have been cast in this form and was thus a ceremonial rather than a utilitarian weapon.

94 A *jar associated with skeleton b* (M XII) lying near the left knee, portraying a marriage of the gods, apparently on a temple-terrace approached by a flight of steps.

95 A *grey-black flask deposited with skeleton c* (M XII) with the same motif as that from coffin *a* in grave E I *(70),* a spiral in relief. This is undoubtedly a symbol, and the most characteristic single element of the Mochica style.

The connection between M XII and E I is emphasized by a squat dark-grey flask found by the head of skeleton *c,* with a second example of the relief of a snake-girded god. The subdivision of his snake girdle is the same as on the serpent-like shelled creatures seen on the E I skirt *(72, 73),* which in turn relates to the jar with the snake relief *(68, 69 above)* found with burial *g* in the same grave.

96 Grave M XII was *unusually rich in copper objects.* I have listed above many finds from the chamber and their numbers increased in the western section of the tomb. Copper bands, sheet, discs and utensils of a luminous green were numerous, especially against the back wall near the heads of the skeletons, where we also found copper head ornaments like those shown in Mochica vase-painting.

One of the most interesting pieces was what one might

97 call a *nose and mouth mask:* the crescent-shaped part would cover the mouth and the upper part the nose. Other pieces of copper which have been found on or between the lips of the dead come to mind. The nose and mouth mask is a pure Mochica invention, known from many Mochica paintings, where it is rendered in chocolate-brown. Only since the M XII find have we realized that a copper mask is intended. It remains an open question whether other painting in this colour, on the feet and hands, also betokens copper. The dark colour may, alternatively, refer to the gods of the night. The grave-goods show that chamber tomb M XII represents a massive Mochica intrusion, with late Chavinoid influences, into a here less preponderant Gallinazo substratum. Alien pottery is included however (fig. 3, left) which is yet older than the Chavín reminiscences of pls *68, 69,* namely a simple jar with incised triangles on the shoulder and with the base of the spout lightly notched where it meets the handle. W. Duncan Strong designated this piece 'Guañape', which would put it alongside Cupisnique/Chavín Costeño chronologically. This will hardly date the whole tomb, though it shows how the otherwise earlier style persisted into early Mochica times.

The third chamber tomb at the lowest level at Pacatnamú, M XI, contained a series of seventeen coarse bulbous Gallinazo pots associated with a stirrup jar with classical Mochica painting (fig. 6). As in E I and M XII the stirrup jar is representative of a small number of high-quality imports found among the predominant, but less competent, local pottery made for burial deposits. The import determines the date of this tomb complex, at latest in the third or fourth century AD.

From the start of excavations in 1937 it was intended to determine the various periods of construction and the different brick forms used in them. The results of our three campaigns have been summarized above (see also Doering 1959, p. 6). During the second campaign two north-south cuttings were made across one of the smaller pyramids, H. 14, revealing four consecutive clay floors dividing five horizons. Below the oldest the natural ground was covered with a thick layer of llama dung. The first visitors from the mountains had brought their animals with them for transport and sacrifice (Doering, 1960, p. 169 ff.).

Pacatnamú: Construction

A complete survey of the structures at Pacatnamú gives a total of fifty-seven pyramids. Flat rectangular and plano-convex ('hemispherical') bricks are found (the latter seen on the right in pl. *98,* in the north wall of H. 31). There is however no tapia, or crushed clay 'concrete', such as is preserved in the impressive ruins of Jatanca *(109),* or 'clod' (irregular lumpy) bricks found in the east wall of the acropolis *(107, below).* Nor are there any conical bricks, like the small narrow ones built into the same wall at Jatanca *(107, above)* and in the 'snake mound' near Tecapa *(114).* Cone bricks are characteristic in coastal Chavín building, and usual (according to Bennett) in Gallinazo work. Their absence at Pacatnamú supports the assumption that our grey jar with relief decoration of a snake-encircled god *(68, 69)* arrived here not from the coast but from another centre where the Chavín tradition still persisted.

In our campaign of 1962-63 we concentrated on terrace H. 31 and the smaller pyramid H. 16. This last, the central structure of a typical Pacatnamú complex of pyramid with eastern and southern outworks, was trenched to ground level. My collaborator, the architect Wolfgang Hecker, also established a 100-metre grid to cover the city and a central bench mark was set up for future measurements. The *terrace H. 31* was examined further by the excavation 98 of the *north front and the approach ramp.* It was remarkable how much was preserved under the protection of débris (compare the aerial photograph in pl. *57).* This shot was taken from the north-east, looking across from the high pyramid H. 12. The plano-convex bricks of later periods

Fig. 6. Vase painting in the Mochica style from grave M XI at Pacatnamú.

are clearly visible in the western section of the north wall, to the right of the ramp. The older base of flat bricks *(56)* lies in the shadow and is partly hidden by the parallel wall. A detail not yet understood is a deep and carefully constructed ditch crossing between the upper end of the ramp and the northern wall of the terrace, but not quite reaching the terrace, with a break about 10 ft. wide. It was obvious from a line of what appear to be geometric ideograms engraved on its face that the smooth grey terrace wall had originally stood free.

99 When the *dividing ditch was cleared* (there were heavy branches in the filling) a smooth line of clay was encountered, terminated to the west by a high brick wall running across the ditch, another incomprehensible feature. The eastern half of the clay floor was cut through and at a depth of 14 ft. we came on another wall, quite distinct from any seen before. It was very low and built of weathered stone, and followed a course different from the east-west orientation of the other walls. It stood on the natural gravel-rock surface of the plateau, the oldest construction on the site. Only further excavation can determine its cultural and chronological setting.

Graves of the fisher folk

In the centre of the northern wall of terrace H. 31 we had reached the earliest pre-Mochica occupation on the plateau of Pacatnamú. In the terrace precincts bordered by the western half of the north wall and the ramp (on the right in pl. *98*) we encountered post-Mochica finds. There were extended burials, completely unrelated to the chamber tombs discovered east of the ramp. The pottery found was quite distinct and simple, but there was a wealth of bright textiles. Among the grave offerings there was almost invariably fishing gear, especially nets with a great variety in the types of knotting. We have called the burials 'graves of the fisher folk'.

Something of their beliefs can be inferred from the worked and painted textiles which emerged as we cleared the débris, like bouquets of bright flowers.

A *fragment of a head* in grey clay, found in the débris near 100 another clay head fragment in the Gallinazo style, is evidence of earlier occupation of this area (some thousand years before the fisher graves by people whose culture must have been related to that associated with the chamber tombs.

A *painted sea scene* showing rowers in reed boats, fisher- 101 men crossing the surf. The massive zig-zag line which divides the rising and falling boats makes it clear that it is not merely pictorial; this is a hieroglyph representing the sea, with its breakers and spray. The rowers themselves are not human fishermen. They are spirits fighting their way to the 'other side', the unattainable 'beyond' of ancient Peruvian thought. They are bird people with bird heads crowned with the great feather helmets characteristic of these later centuries. There is only one possibly human figure, under the wave and shown with a pointed cap, in a manner typical of this art. He is perhaps an ideogram, denoting the connection between the world of the dead and the sea which gives sustenance to fishermen.

Mythical sea scenes on painted cloth are not uncommon in the fisher-graves at Pacatnamú. But they are rare on the woven cloths, the slit (kelim) tapestries.

102 *Slit tapestry excavated in the field of the fisher-folk.* This first example found in 1962 is a fragment of a long band with multicoloured two-headed bird-creatures, the so-called 'double eagles'. We may dismiss the idea that the bird figures were intended for use in a strip as they were woven (our band was found rolled up); instead they were divided along the narrow gaps between the motifs and then sewn individually on to mantles or covers in a chess-board pattern. A fragment of such a mantle was discovered in the fisher-grave region in 1962, and pl. *103* illustrates another figure which was evidently intended for similar appliqué work.

The significance of the 'double eagle' is unknown. Its discovery at Pacatnamú, however, raises a problem. Stylized two-headed bird-figures entirely similar to those from the region of the fisher folk graves had already been found on the coast about 375 miles further south at Pachacamac, near Lima, which was still a centre of pilgrimage in Inca times. Both the Berlin Museum and the Gaffron collection at the Chicago Art Institute contain a series of applied 'double eagles' from Pachacamac, and they had been con-sidered (Schmidt, 1929) as peculiar to this site. From the fact that our Pacatnamú examples were scientifically excavated, however, while those known as from Pachacamac were collected decades before by treasure-seekers who had every inducement to conceal the true area of their activities, I am personally inclined to believe that those examples actually came from Pacatnamú. Against this suggestion is the absence up till now at our site of tapestry finds showing fish figures, like those in the Pachacamac collections. This seems strange among fishing folk, and the problem remains unsolved, to await further excavation at Pacatnamú. In any case it is impossible that two such similar figures could occur independently on sites some 375 miles apart. They originated either at Pachacamac or at Pacatnamú, or alternatively both tapestries came from a third (unknown) site.

There is a similar though less obvious problem concerning *picture cloths showing gods* under the canopy of a starry sky. 103 A god stands full-face holding up sceptres between two officiating priests with animal heads. It is as though light is radiating from the region of the stars. It is impossible to mistake the Tiahuanaco style in the forceful representation, as in the well-known central figure on the sun gate at Tiahuanaco itself.

TECAPA - JATANCA

The ruins of old cities and temple mounds are found not only on the edge of valleys, where ancient groves of huarango protect the fields against drifting sand; they also lie beyond in the often shadowless desert, disappearing beneath shifting dunes to reappear when the dunes move on.

104 This is best seen from a height of a several hundred feet, as here at *Jatanca, a ruined city in the northern Paiján desert (pampa)*. In the centre is the city, partly covered by dunes up to 30 ft. in height. Above to the left, where a dark zapote bush just manages to stay alive, is a flat mound called the acropolis on account of its commanding position above the dunes (see also pl. *106, above*). At the bottom right is an isolated building in the arm of a dune, which was important for measuring the rate at which the dunes moved. This photograph was taken when we flew over the site in April 1963; the dune was then approaching the structure, but when I returned in October of the same year to make a sketch-map of the building the dune had encroached to cover half of it, a distance of 25 yards in six months. Allowing for the possibility that the building slowed down the movement of the sand we can accept the average rate of the dune's advance as about 60 yards a year (Kinzl, 1958, p. 11).

105 Viewed from the ground the *sickle-shaped dunes* look like breakers in the sea. On the top right edge of the plate the Jatanca acropolis is visible. On the left edge appear the first thorny trees of the huarango forest which contains the desert city of Tecapa. Nearby is our first camp set up in the lee of a dune. The photograph was taken looking towards the south, the direction from which the dunes are approaching.

Jatanca and the much later city of Tecapa are quite distinct from each other in construction. At Jatanca *(109) tapia,* or cast crushed clay, construction predominates and

106 it also occurs at the *Jatanca acropolis* (here looking from ▲ north to south) in walls in front of the north foot and on

106 the *heights of the acropolis* in walls enclosing small intercon- ▼ necting rooms.

Tapia construction is again found in the east wall of the acropolis, both as a base below, and as an extension above

107 the roughly worked *conical bricks* which are set on end, ▲ built up with clay fragments and clay mortar between.

107 Sections of such walls alternate here with *walls of 'clod'* ▼ *bricks,* which bring to mind the polygonal stone walls of the mountain zone (e.g. Tarahuasi, Andénes near Chincheros etc.).

A *flight of nine steps high on the acropolis* is also flanked on *108* one side by conical bricks, while the other is made up of ▲ unusually large, flat rectangular ones. I had hoped to expose a ramp at this spot; instead these steps appeared from beneath the débris, 7 ft. wide and 1 ft. 6 in. deep, in an excellent state of preservation.

Several *sherds lay on the acropolis steps,* of which two had *108* the negative painting characteristic of the Gallinazo style, ▼ which is so significant for identification. There was also an example of the decoration described as 'triangular punctuations... in pendant triangles bordered by incised lines' in an American publication of Virú valley finds of the Gallinazo period (Ford, 1949, p. 75: 'an uncommon variant' of 'Castillo incised ware'), as well as two fragments with incised angular lines, such as were found in excavations at Chavín de Huantar (Bennett, 1944, fig. 29, o). I found similarly ornamented sherds in cemeteries near the Hacienda Ocucaje in the Ica valley, where they belonged with Paracas Cavernas finds. Thus the steps were, so to speak, unequivocally labelled as of an early period.

In the *city of Jatanca tapia walls* are made from huge blocks, *109* some 6 ft. long, of crushed clay pressed or moulded together. At this time the sand had blown clear of these walls, though they would soon be covered again.

There were no outstanding pieces among the pottery finds in the city of Jatanca, but the acropolis yielded an unusual fragment of a *demon face with the eye surrounded by a snake, 110* which does not connect with any known style. From the same site came a *head of a beast of prey on the neck of an urn 111* which may be interpreted as a Chavinoid relic if not in true Chavín style.

Fragment of a face from the Jatanca acropolis. The eyes and *112* mouth appear to have been indicated by a narrow wooden ▲ wedge.

Fragment of a clay face from the same site, with the mouth *112* again composed of two wedge impressions and the eyes ▼ of a hollow ring. Both these fragments can be included in the Gallinazo style, which flourished on the site before the Mochica. The numerous sherds from the acropolis included only one or two per cent. in Mochica style.

A small mound which stands in the vicinity of Tecapa may nonetheless be independent of that city and more closely related to the Jatanca acropolis. We named it the 'snake mound', after the fragment of a large red *urn with snakes 113 in relief* below the rim. Their sinuous bodies are impressed with white spots; the heads lay below the out-curve of the shoulder and had been broken off. Writhing spotted snakes are not unknown on pottery, but there is nothing to compare with these splendid fragments. To judge from other finds in the mound they should be dated around the first century AD or later.

114 This date is supported by the peculiar *conical bricks*, which look like pointed hats. Some of them are built into the low remains of a wall, with their flat bases vertical to form the wall face, as in the Chavín Punkurí temple in the Nepeña valley, or the Cerro Sechín temple in the Casma valley *(167)*. The snake mound has the closest relations of the Tecapa-Jatanca area with the first great horizon style of ancient Peru, the Chavín style.

Although the cities of Jatanca and Tecapa are so near geographically they are obviously chronologically quite distinct. Between the beginning of Jatanca, lying in the open desert *(104)* and the end of the huarango-encircled city of Tecapa *(116)* fifteen hundred years may have elapsed. This conclusion is supported by the different building techniques, and by pottery finds. The survivors

115 of Jatanca apparently took over *Tecapa, in the shelter of the trees,* when their city was submerged by sand, until the encroaching dunes drove them out yet again.

Building technique shows that Tecapa is relatively more

116 recent. The *walls at Tecapa* are built of rectangular adobe bricks laid with thick mortar between, recalling the late walls of Pacatnamú. Peculiar to the site are squared pillars or columns of adobe; these are represented here and there by their bases, or even preserved in part at times in rows. The west side of pyramid I at Pacatnamú also produced a row of squared pillar bases, which probably supported a roofed hall. In the farther reaches of the city are the cultivated areas of Tecapa, with their meandering irrigation canals still clearly recognizable *(43)*.

The most recent pottery (which includes Inca) in the Tecapa-Jatanca region was found on the 'potters' mound' on the northern limits of Tecapa; the earliest finds – Cupisnique, Cupisnique Transitorio, 'Ancon Brushed' (Ford, 1949, p. 77), Gallinazo and unclassified early styles – occurred on the snake mound and on the southern edge of Jatanca, on the acropolis. Only on the 'potters' mound'

are Inca sherds found near Gallinazo examples, and this because the site, on the edge of the desert and apparently near a good source of clay, was in use for centuries, as numerous sherds and spoiled pieces show. By removing the intervening sand, wind action has destroyed any true stratigraphy.

The chronological sequence can be traced from south to north: on the acropolis only one or two per cent. of Mochica sherds among the early styles; to the north, across the Tecapa desert, the Mochica percentage increases until further north still it is submerged by Cajamarca cursive, Chimú and finally Inca-style fragments. This 'horizontal stratigraphy' is the most reliable guide to interpreting these wind-swept sites (Woolley).

A *head found in the desert sand,* the eyes treated in early 117 Mochica style (and reminiscent of an early Greek goddess of the sixth century).

An example of a *head* in an even more pronounced later 118 Mochica style. ▲

A *badly weathered head,* the eyes recalling the upward slant 118 of the treatment found in the Lambayeque style (north ▼ Peru).

A *typical Mochica head* with individual characterization. 119

Two small heads recovered from the sand which has deeply pitted their surface. These highly individual heads are amongst the most expressive of the (mostly larger) 120 clay models. For the appreciation of the fine detail the photographs have been enlarged.

A *parrot head* from the Tecapa desert, still in the Gallinazo 121 style (the applied 'button' eyes resemble the example in ▲ pl. *112, below*).

Head of a 'tiger-man' in Mochica style, in which representa- 121 tions of this creature, half man and half tiger, are not ▼ infrequently found. They recall the Amazon Indian belief that witch-doctors turn into jaguars – the American tigers – when they die.

Spindles and needles found in the sand at Tecapa. The eye 122 of the needle is formed from a tongue-like extension of the shank.

CUPISNIQUE

123 *Stone flake tools from the Cupisnique, or Mocan, desert* in north Peru take us back nine or ten thousand years, to early man in South America *(123–127)*. The curved points in the top row – 'shark's teeth' – are matched by examples from the Danger Cave, Utah, with a C-14 age of 11,300 years (Jennings, 1953, lower right in fig. 1 and pp. 185, 186). We first found artefacts of palaeolithic character near Cupisnique (situated in desert country north of the Chicama valley) in 1933 and we returned there in 1937 and 1953.

The find-site is a stony desert, consisting of two wide and *124* flat valley depressions divided by the rocky *Cerro Colorado* near the Cupisnique ravine, and *the more easterly 'road valley'*, which contains the route to the ravine. We found numerous sherds in the coastal Chavín style called Cupisnique by Rafael Larco Hoyle. Stone artefacts, by contrast, were concentrated in the western valley (left in the upper photograph in pl. *124*), the 'lake valley', which had, according to the geological research of Dr Welter, originated as a lake bed. When this dried out a small river cut a broad path through its bed, forming a second horizon;

through this in turn it cut a narrower and deeper channel, the third horizon. Fossil bones of the South American diluvial period – the water-hog *Neochoerus* and the armadillo *Pampatherium*, according to Professor Dehm of *125-127* Munich – and artefacts of *palaeolithic type* are found together on the upper terrace. The occasional tools found at lower levels had been transported there. The stone tools and fossils are further related by a covering of desert lac; while the scattered sherd finds from all three horizons are with one exception without it.

None of our finds was buried in the ground, only covered with blown sand. Earlier covering layers would have been carried away by the wind; an exploratory cut to 18 in. beneath the fossil bones and artefacts confirmed that nothing else lay concealed in the ground.

In 1937 I found a deposit of human bones in the 'lake valley'. Professor Mollison of Munich University pronounced them to be of an unusually slender type, either adolescent or perhaps representing a more delicate race than is now standard in South America. It is even possible that these human remains belong to hunters who lived in the then wooded valleys during the softer climate of the north Peruvian diluvial.

HUACA CAMPANA

The very different surroundings in which we find burials with Mochica material are illustrated by a stone grave in a
128 pyramid of *adobe and rough stones* built like a look-out terrace on a rocky mountain spur in the upper valley of the Chicama. This structure has also a historical significance: it was passed by Alexander von Humboldt a hundred and fifty years ago on his journey through Ecuador to Trujillo and Lima. The promontory on which the 'Huaca Campana' is built gives no clue that Mochica graves might be found up there; nor are there many instances of burials in pyramids. It is as yet undecided whether the Campana pyramid was a burial pyramid. The grave offerings in our Campana grave are in pure Mochica style.

129 This *fragment of a head* (part of a jar), with warm dark-brown painting over matt white, is characteristic. It is no portrait (as is the head in pls *158, 159*), but represents a generalized type, with an animal head as a crest or badge over the brow. To judge from its spots the animal is apparently a jaguar.

The difficulty of excavating among sharp broken rocks which made up the body of the pyramid can be seen from
130 this *pottery jar surrounded by stones* over the grave's beamed roof (*barbacoa*), as though cemented there. Surprisingly the jar was undamaged, showing how carefully the infill was laid. Above to the right a small pottery offering (illustrated in pl. *132, below*) is visible under large blocks in the heap of stone.

In still greater danger of damage from its covering of
131 broken rock is a *figurine jar* lying under shattered stones
▼ and bones. It had nonetheless been possible to deposit the
131 *figurine in a cavity unharmed,* and it stood upright in the
▲ grave as though rising from the dead. In the right hand it holds up a shield and a club in the left. There is a helmet

on the head in the form of a crouching jaguar, perhaps as a form of protection, with raised claws and open jaws, turned to face the intruder. The disc ear-rings are hung from the ear, and not attached by piercing the lobe.

The skeleton lay extended (the bones much decayed) from south to north like the Pacatnamú burials, under a cover of beams which are now perceptible only as lines of brown mould. *Small globular pots, probably for drink offerings* were *132* encountered throughout and were a characteristic feature ▼ of the grave.

A *painted stirrup-handled jar from the Campana grave.* Painted *132* above the crabs in relief ane water plants, with waves of ▲ the sea round the base and on the spout and handle.

Another grave offering – and another invocation of water, and so concerned with fertility – is a *figure of a frog.* Only *133* the large head with its bulging eyes is preserved. The painting, which is rarely absent on Mochica pottery, is again in dark chestnut brown on a milk-white ground. Water was also the concern of the artist in the symbols on a *deep goblet or bowl with water birds and rosettes* of leaves *134* from water plants. Among the few unpainted jars was a figure of a *drummer girl,* holding the drum on a band under *135 r* the right arm, and a remarkable little figure of a *warrior* *135 l* *in a typical Mochica helmet* with large disc ear-rings, resting or climbing on a shallow drum.

Perhaps the most original find in the Campana grave was a *clay Janus-like head,* moulded and hollow inside like a *136* libation vessel. The mouth is covered by a crescent-shaped mask, like that found combined with a nose mask in grave M XII at Pacatnamú (*97*). The significance of this head is unknown. This example does not represent the opposition of life and death as do models in ancient Mexico. One head would then have been a skull. The find is another encounter with the religious world of the Mochica which we do not understand.

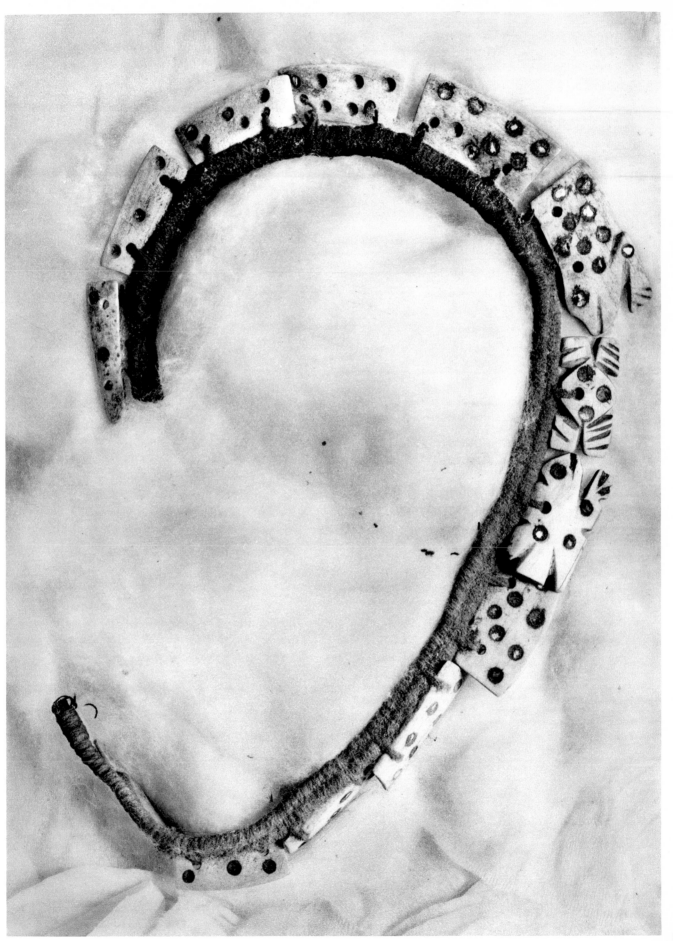

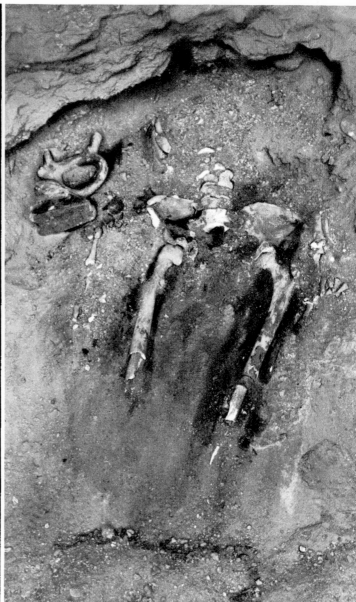

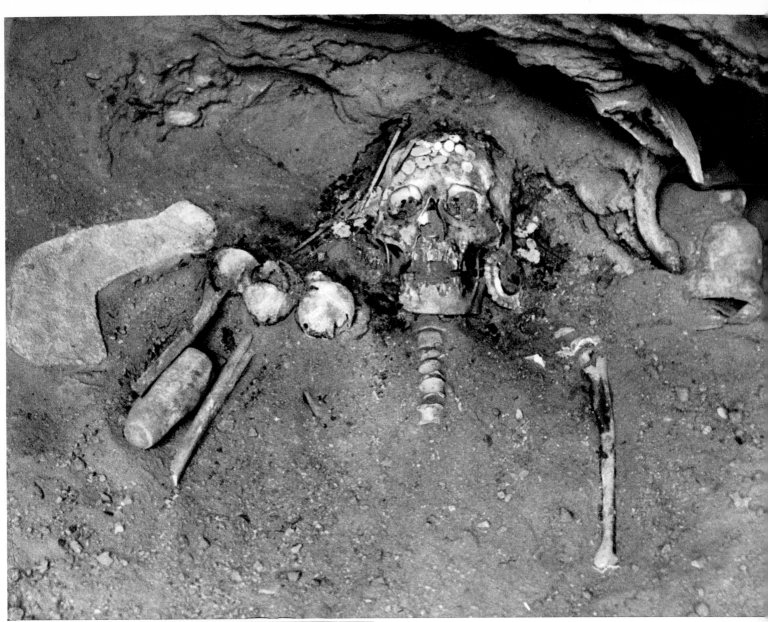

 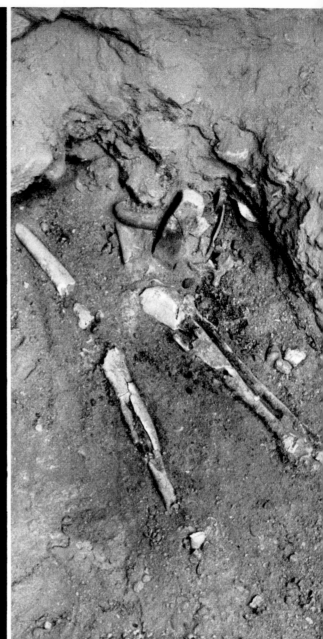

108

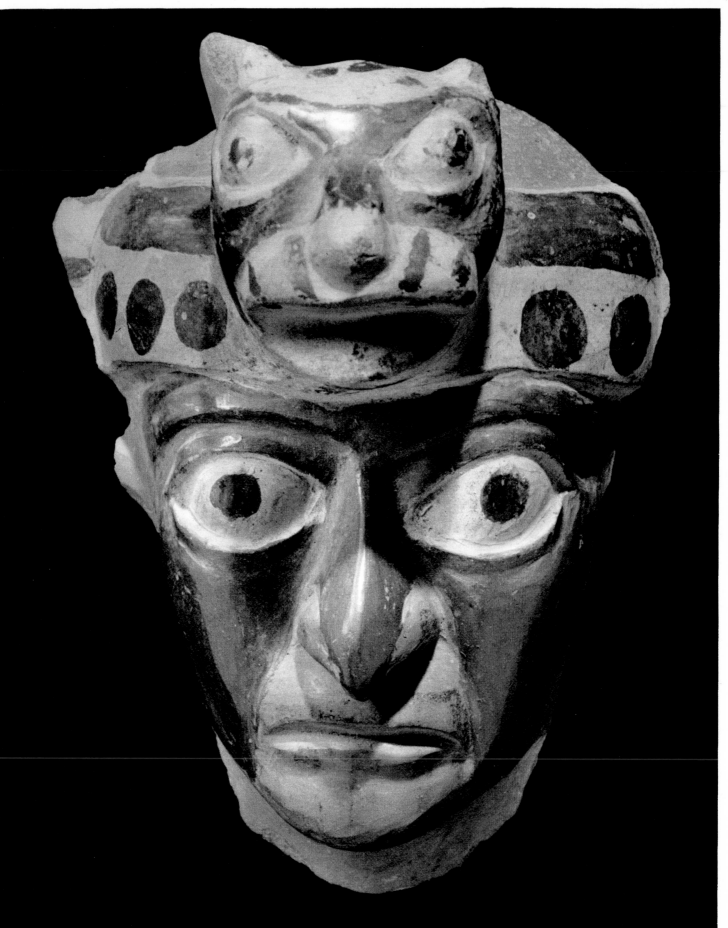

135

135

136

THE MOCHE PYRAMIDS

145 One of the largest monuments in the Peruvian coast-lands is the *sun pyramid near Moche* in northern Peru, which is over 130 ft. high. Mochica architects contributed to its construction, though they are responsible not for the mighty facing which gives the pyramid its form today but for the much smaller central structure, part of which must have come to light when treasure-seekers in colonial times diverted the river Moche up to the pyramid in the hope of finding riches in the centre. Among other things they found wall-paintings in the central part of the pyramid, showing people with 'moustaches'. These will have been either the crescent-shaped masks like those on the head from Huaca Campana *(136)* or a moustache-emblem like that on the upper lip of the head from terrace H. 31 at Pacatnamú *(59)*. At all events they were paintings in Mochica style.

146 The *sun pyramid at Moche* is built from a multitude of flat
147 bricks. On the *river side where it has been broken open* it can be seen that these are not laid in continuous horizontal courses but in massive vertical blocks of different sizes, built up against each other and not always on a level footing. There are no plano-convex or conical bricks at this site.

148 Remnants of *wall-painting in Mochica style* are preserved on the ruins of a small building near the Moche moon pyramid (see below). The incised outlines of the legs of two running figures are visible painted in white, yellow, dark ochre, brick red, pale blue and black. The remaining portion measured 2 ft. 6 in. high by nearly 4 ft. wide in 1932. I have no idea how it has fared, lying exposed to the weather, the sea-wind and to tourists.

149 The second great pyramid at Moche, the *moon pyramid (Huaca de la Luna)* by contrast appears to be entirely of Mochica construction. Built at the foot of a granite mountain (the Cerro Blanco) it is a great stepped terrace rather than a pyramid. It stands nearly 70 ft. high, built of large adobe bricks which are much thinner than those in the sun pyramid. Often they carry fluted impressions of reeds on their narrower sides. Max Uhle's excavations of Mochica graves, which were fundamental for the chronological interpretation of north Peruvian culture, took place on the ground in front of the moon terrace.

While classical Mochica culture did not last beyond AD 500, the celebrated ruined city of Chan-Chan, with its so-called palaces and wall engravings (reaching 450 yards by 375 yards in size) belongs to the thirteenth to fifteenth centuries, at least in its visible portions. A pre-Chimú Chan-Chan, however, must underlie these ruins, *150* and a *copper relief plaque* from the site is evidence of it. The decorative plaque is in two parts with four opposed motifs, like fleshy commas, on the common central field; this is a pattern or symbol known in Mochica vase painting, where it appears as a badge on a sort of pouch used for documents, at times paired, as on half of the Chan-Chan plaque. There is still some underground stone construction at Chan-Chan in a style alien to Chimú which was exposed by past treasure-seekers. But there is not necessarily a complete pre-Chimú city left covered over for the archaeologist to discover; earlier buildings may have been carried off, or cleared away, when the present Chan-Chan was built.

151 *Chan-Chan, the city of the Chimú,* cannot have arisen without precursors. It must rest on the site of an older centre. In the last century before the Spanish invasion half of Peru was ruled from this city, a coastal realm over 600 miles long between Tumbez on the gulf of Guayaquil in the north to the region of Lima in the south. The encircling 'palace' wall, with newer building near its top, reaches 25 ft. in height and is supported at fixed intervals by built-in upright posts of carob wood, doubtless against the not infrequent earthquakes. The great square-walled site in the foreground of pl. *151* shows two parallel walls enclosing the palace wall, with a long narrow passage between them.

Chan-Chan became renowned not only for its gold treasures, which came to light during the colonial centuries, but for its *rich and widespread relief work.* Unfortu- *152, 153* nately it must be stated that the reliefs illustrated no longer exist. The photographs were taken fifty years ago by Frau Caecilie Seler-Sachs, wife of the great Americanist Eduard Seler, to whom I am indebted for their use in the plates. The reliefs remind one of wall carpets, which they doubtless replaced, that is of textiles similar to those found in the graves of the fisher folk at Pacatnamú. In particular the broad sinuous wave-like bands filled with fishes and crabs are comparable with the scenes painted on these textiles *(101).*

Fisher-spirits and rowers, birds, fish and other sea creatures cover the walls in symbolic or magical bands, and between are chess-board patterns of little cubes (in the background in pl. *152).* Damp air from the nearby sea and the very occasional falls of rain did much to obscure the reliefs once they were freed from their protective covering of clay. And they are now exposed to ever-growing numbers of tourists.

TYPICAL POTTERY

Some illustrations are included as examples typifying the frequently mentioned Chimú, Mochica and Chavín styles.

154, 155 A *large grey globular vessel in Chimú style* with two opposed hemispherical cappings of relief ornament, showing flocks of circling aquatic birds driven by four-footed animals round the borders. From a site *(huaca)* in the Virú valley near the sea, where one might well hear the cries of a whirling mass of birds above the surf.

156, 157 A *painted stirrup-jar representative of the Mochica style*. The central figure in the mythical scene is a god with club and shield, half encircled by radiating serpent-headed shafts. His helmet bears the typical Mochica crescent device. The dark tones of his face denote a superhuman character. The entreating figure with an offering in his hands in front of him is perhaps a priest, like the one standing higher to the right, under the handle, who appears to be approaching the warrior in an attitude of submission. The fighting figures in the lively scenes are wearing bird- and fox-masks, or sometimes they storm across the stage with only their clubs, an established motif in ancient Peruvian mythology. The enemy is dragged along by the hair with great gusto. The grasping of the hair is a conventional Mochica representation of victor and vanquished. The victims are led to a dreadful fate, which they seem to know awaits them. As in all Mochica painting the colours are brown on white. The clay is unglazed, like all pre-Columbian pottery in America.

If the Mochica palette was limited, there is a wealth of sculptural form in Mochica art. Mochica modelling is renowned and includes portrait-heads which must be of individual persons, dating from the first half-century AD.

An *outstanding portrait-head* (from a private collection in *158, 159* Peru) in Mochica style, bought near Chimbote. The exact origin of this remarkable work remains unknown, but the Mochica inspiration can be recognized with certainty. We do not understand the significance of the dark painting on part of the face. It may have reference to the realm of the dead.

The third and oldest, the Chavín style, we have already encountered in late examples, the relief vase and demon head in pls. *68, 69*, and in the similar fragment in pl. *110*. Typical works are a *black graphite stirrup-jar with Chavín- 160 Costeño characteristics*: stroke ornament in zones between relief work in powerful curves (Chavín could also be called the 'curved' or 'tiger' style). This example has a heavy stirrup handle and a voluminous spout with encircling lip.

A *black graphite vase in the shape of a standing monkey* with *161* impressed dots covering the body; the modelling is emphasized by deep incisions, for example in the bend of the arms and round the eyes. The open mouth forms the spout. The hollow body of this jar is again heavy in construction; but the legs and tail are in perfect proportion, a composition of the first order. (These last two pieces are now preserved in the Museo Nacional de Arqueología in Lima.)

CERRO BLANCO

162, 163 Remains of the *Cerro Blanco temple* in the Nepeña valley south of Chimbote, which belongs in the 'tiger' or 'curved' Chavín style. The ornamentation consists of a row of repeated red-on-white motifs with deeply incised outline:

the powerful incisors of the tiger god, like dagger or sword blades, representing his whole head. This is pure Chavín style. These wonderful curves were decorating a temple step when I took the photograph in 1953. Nothing could be found of them when I searched the débris which alone remained in 1963.

QUISQUE

From the type-site of Chavín de Huantar, on the eastern slopes of the Cordillera Blanca, westward along the Nepeña and Casma valleys to the coast between Trujillo and Lima a zone of typically Chavín stone building can be traced, in a region where brick construction predominates.

164 The cyclopean *temple citadel of Quisque* belongs in this zone; it is built on a rocky height above the Nepeña valley, like many large buildings in ancient Peru it appears never to have been finished.

In the intense heat of the southern summer it is a strenuous climb over loose rocks *(164, above)* to reach the massive outer wall, but the sight of its corner draws one irresistibly on, and on arrival it is obvious that the effort was not in vain. The wall *(164, below)* consists of smoothed granite blocks of varying sizes, some measuring as much as six by nine feet and three feet thick; they are especially large at the corners *(166)*. At the corners and around the entrance *(166* and *165, below)* the dressed blocks are levelled to horizontal by thin slabs and loose stone. Such construction recalls the temple at Chavín (Bennett, 1944, pl. 6 B and 7 D) and one is tempted to see in the Quisque structure

a cruder copy of the walls of the Huantar temple. Reliefs and sculptures in stone, however, are absent (at least nowadays) at Quisque, though sherd finds are comparable at the two places.

The *wall between the entrances* is irregularly built from large *165* broken rocks, at times with rounded surfaces. This length of wall resembles somewhat stretches at Callejón de Huaylas in the upper Santa valley.

That the Quisque citadel was primarily a temple is shown by *sacred granite cliffs* which had to be enclosed by walls. *165* However, the plan was only partly put into effect, and building material is still lying about the site. The site of Ollantaytambo comes to mind. G. E. Squier recognized long ago that its cliffs were sacred (1883, p. 258). It is possible that Quisque centred round these sacred rocks. There are irregular blocks of granite lying about on a flat space inside the walls which perhaps enjoyed the respect and veneration which the Andean people used to give to great rocks and cliffs.

The *north-east corner of the encircling wall* of the Quisque *166* temple citadel showing its commanding site above the Nepeña valley and the Andean character of the stone construction.

CERRO SECHÍN

167 The *temple of Cerro Sechín* in the Casma valley (the next valley south of the Nepeña) has recently become famous for its reliefs carved on upright monolithic slabs. The slabs stand separated in a row in front of the lower of two temple terraces.

167 Also included in the structures at *Cerro Sechín* are *conical bricks* placed on edge so that their circular bases contribute to the wall surface, as in the little Chavín temple of Punkurí in the Nepeña valley and in wall fragments in the Tecapa snake mound. Thus in structure the Cerro Sechín temple could belong to a Chavín-influenced group on the coast.

The Sechín reliefs *(168–171)* however are *sui generis* and have nothing to do with the Chavín style. They are so far unique and unrelated to any other Peruvian art. The Cerro Blanco reliefs *(162, 163)* are drawn consistently and in a highly developed style recognizable in every line and detail. The Sechín reliefs are quite different, giving the impression of formlessness, without being formless. For these reliefs also obey stylistic rules, different as they are from those at Cerro Blanco. There is scarcely anything which

could be ascribed to the Chavín style; there is no trace of the there dominant tiger god, with his predator's teeth and claws and unmistakable eyes. It is only outside Peru that one can find similar figures, in the famous 'dancers' on the Monte Alban in Mexico.

The *dancers of Cerro Sechín* are unmistakably similar to *168, 169* the Mexican examples, if not in every detail then in the general aspect of the figures. (The outline of the figure has unfortunately been drawn over by a visitor.) W. Bennett (1954, p. 34) sees the Sechín relief as evidence of a new and early style assuming (though without stratigraphical proof) it to be older than the Chavín.

A detail alike on the dancers and the *warriors on the Cerro* *170* *Sechín reliefs* which must have some special significance is the strikingly long, almost dagger-like thumbnail. The finger nails do not extend beyond the finger tips.

On smaller stones between the monolithic slabs are incised representations of human heads (shown as dead with closed eyes), which are without question *trophy heads*. *171* Many of the heads have bands rising from the mouth and by analogy with the conventions of medieval painting we may surmise that they denote a cry rising from the spell-laden head, or a sacred song.

LOCARÍ

Having considered the oldest, and pre-Christian, horizon style, the Chavín, and its monuments we turn at Locarí in the Huayurí valley (the most northerly tributary of the Nazca) to burials of the second half of the first century AD with grave offerings in the Tiahuanaco style, or the second of the horizon styles in ancient Peru. The pottery and textile decoration is severely stylized, often called geometric. This style can to a large degree have been determined by translating woven pictures and ornament into stone relief work. The best example of such a translation is the great relief on the sun gate at Tiahuanaco.

The people responsible for the Locarí graves came to the coast from the mountains, overthrowing the older coastal population who were condemned to labour and to provide the sacrifices required by the funeral rites of the conquerors.

172, 173 At the centre of the small cemetery was the *grave of a chieftain or valley king* with a crouched burial facing south, as in all southern Tiahuanaco graves and their derivatives; this is in marked contrast to the north-facing burials at Pacatnamú and Campana. In this valley south remained the sacred direction up to the time of the Spaniards.

The grave was a rectangular pit with a cover of logs *(barbacoa)* on which a layer of stones and leaves *(torta)* was thrown. An upright stone slab was let into the south wall as an entrance door, and the pottery offerings placed outside it (recalling the arrangement at the sacred rocks at Lacco in the Cuzco region). All the Tiahuanaco-Costeño burials in this cemetery were of bodies lying or sitting in similar graves, while the graves of earlier inhabitants consisted of narrow cylindrical shafts.

The dead man in this chieftain's grave did not go to the other world alone. At his side (left) sit as sacrifices two apparently female corpses (one has fallen forward), and there were several small children with very fine head cloths to the right near his feet and near the shoulder in pls. *172, 173.*

The chieftain was wrapped in a *woollen mantle with typical motifs (symbols) in the Coast Tiahuanaco style*: the heads of predatory beasts between bands of volutes or frets (meanders). This is a magical symbol complex rendered in seven colours, red, pink, yellow, yellow-brown, brown, grey and light green with black; the ground is dyed in ochre-gold. The dead man wore no crown, helmet or head-binding. His black hair fell down over his face. The grave was completely undisturbed. When we lifted the carefully cleared cover the occupants were *in situ*, veiled by the dust of a thousand years. Pottery was placed at the feet of the dead man and to the left a jar in the shape of a *demon crab*. If this may be regarded as an example of Tiahuanaco style, the more so were two handled beakers ('Roman', though without a foot) which were identical with finds from Tiahuanaco itself.

A *burial shaft for human sacrifices* a few yards south-west of the main grave. It was filled with skeletons, powdered clay and stones. The grave measured 3 ft. across by 6 ft. in depth and contained the jumbled bones and skulls of eleven individuals. They had been slain and thrown into the grave; the marks of a blow are clearly seen on the top skull on the left. It was recognized that even sacrifices had need of grave offerings of pottery, and the vessels seem to have been interspersed among the bodies.

From Grave VI at Locarí, a Coast Tiahuanaco rectangular pit grave, a *jar with contrasted light and dark painting* on the lower part, a decoration deriving from the traditions of earlier inhabitants of the coast.

The magic the ancients believed immanent in animal figures is still obvious today in the *pottery fish from Grave III at Locarí,* swimming along with staring eyes. A fish was the symbol for the water which was essential to all life. The dead were reminded to entreat for it when they reached the realm of the gods.

174

175

176

177 ▲

177 ▼

The creatures – crab and fish – deposited in the Locarí graves were simple stylized representations. In the large shaft graves on the Morro de Cahuachi (above the Rio Grande de Nazca) we find a different type of mythical beast, a composite animal made up from parts of birds, fish and cats but representative of none of them. They are portrayed because of a belief in the effectiveness of their magical powers.

178 An example of a *mythical beast from grave I at Cahuachi*: ▲ the body is painted in the manner of a fish, with a great forked fish tail; the little fishes swimming about within this outline may be associated with times when water was abundant. This complex beast has four legs which are human and a jaw with teeth. The volutes springing from the fish outline may be cloud symbols; a beam of light shines out from between each pair. At the same time the beast is a jar which may have held a drink-offering. A little stopper still hangs from the spout, attached by a cotton thread.

178 A *hemispherical black bowl* from the same grave I at Cahua- ▼ chi with three round cartouches painted with almost hieroglyphic devices: a volute creature resembling some twisting aquatic animal, a final reminder of the so-called notched-staff demon of the older Nazca painting which preceded that found in these graves. There is no doubt that the figures on the older painting have been reduced in the volutes to ideograms. The red volutes which sprouted and luxuriated in previous Nazca work are here reduced to their essence — they denote fertility.

The black surface of the bowl was applied after firing. There were two such bowls in the grave *(179)* standing one inside the other, just in front of the right-hand post near a trophy head with plaited hair. A maize cob had been placed in the head's lower jaw (as a charm for the growth of the fields) and was held in place by a cloth.

179 *Shaft-grave I at Cahuachi* (which contained pottery in pl. *178)*; this reconstruction was in the Munich Museum and was destroyed in the Second World war. The grave reached a total depth of 12 ft. and consisted of a stepped shaft with the lower part, with a timber cover, as the burial chamber. Remnants show that its four walls were hung with fabrics with stepped patterns rendered in interlocked warp technique. If the steps are interpreted as the rise of the clouds and the fall of rain, it is not fanciful to see the dead man as entreating the clouds. In the centre of the back wall, and wrapped in a great cotton cloth in plain light-blue and pink, was the most remarkable piece of the grave furnishings, the seat of the mummy. It resembled a basket made from bundles of plant stems wrapped round with black cloths and wound into a spiral. Inside the spiral were superimposed layers of black gauze cloth, a great folded net and thick beds of grass, and the whole was covered by the light-coloured cloth. The spiral throne can be regarded as the *Leitfossil* of cemeteries in the middle and southern Nazca valleys, thus belonging to a 'basket grave culture' (also called in Spanish *caracol* graves, from the resemblance of the spirally wound basket seat to a snail shell).

Behind the basket seat are two flat posts of huarango wood. (Similar examples were also found in the still larger grave II at Cahuachi.) The pottery was placed in front of the dead man on a thick layer of pacay leaves (see the mythical beast in pl. *178 above,* which stood in front of the left-hand post). At the front in the corners lay trophy heads with plaited hair over maize cobs; their significance is not clear. Against the back wall on the left is a hemispherical lump of lime; lime plays a part in the chewing of coca leaves. This Morro grave dates from about the fifth to seventh centuries AD.

Cahuachi II was even larger than grave I. The upper shaft tapered downwards from 22 to 18 ft. square, and it was 16 ft. deep.

The *beams covering the burial chamber* consisted of eight 180 strong timbers cut from huarango trunks.

Some of the timbers of *the cover were wrapped in white* 181 *cotton cloth.* In the carefully laid deposit above it a large ▲ cotton cloth had been stretched out over the lowest layer of stones, and *some stones had even been wrapped individually.* 181 The complete beam cover lay under another cloth of ▼ white cotton with colourful brocaded corner ornament (left foreground in pl. *180).*

The richest finds, in quality and number alike, were the textiles. A technique which reached its highest accomplishment here is *interlocked warp pattern* (sometimes called 182 patchwork in English), used in this example for a simple stepped design in brown, grey and white, like the wall-hanging from Cahuachi I *(179).* Each woven field is an entity which is worked into the whole cloth by interlocking the yarns.

A *colourful and highly stylized picture cloth in patchwork* 183 *technique;* like the previous example this fragment is from shaft-grave II at Cahuachi. It is not easy to penetrate the stylization and recognize the original figures. The simplest to interpret is the beast in the centre square on the right; the bird below (with its head to the left) is more difficult.

It requires some familiarity with Peruvian motifs to discern the trophy head at the bottom of the centre column: the eye in the middle is shown open in a new life, under a volute crown and with plaits of hair streaming down towards the left.

Despite disturbance, apparently in early colonial times, shaft-grave II at Cahuachi contained an abundance of most *184* important finds, among them the *brocaded corner ornament* already mentioned on the cloth laid over the chamber cover. These corner brocades are inseparable from the Morro graves and their culture. They are widespread in cemeteries of the Nazca region, like the basket seats of the dead, though they seem to persist later than these. I have never found even a fragmentary example without also encountering the standard associations of pottery and textiles.

Compared with the textiles, pottery in the Morro graves is not particularly remarkable, especially when it is contrasted with the Nazca work of the early centuries AD, *185* which is represented in grave II by *two bowls, with humming-birds and flowers* (above) and perhaps *paprika pods* (below). The first in particular is in classical early Nazca style, the characteristic elements are stylized but without breaking down the objects depicted into abstract patterns. These bowls do not properly belong in a Morro grave; yet the accomplishment of the humming-bird bowl precluded our regarding them as mere survivals. It can more readily be surmised that they were possessions of a subjugated Nazca, which were contributed to the rich grave.

A closer connection between the early Nazca and Morro styles, and the coexistence of the two cultures, can be inferred from a patterned band of dull-green cloth from the large grave II at Cahuachi. It is 5 ft. 6 in. long with numerous multicoloured motifs sketched on in embroidery: flowering plants, birds, insects, possibly fruit and other shapes whose meaning was clear only to those who worked it. Our example did not lend itself to detailed *186, 187* photography; instead two other similar *embroidered bands*, which are perhaps a collection of embroidery patterns, also from the Nazca valleys, are illustrated. Especially on the smaller one *(187)* various birds, plants and perhaps fishes can be recognized, together with other 'jottings' with the needle, which need to be compared with similar examples before they can be identified.

What was the purpose of these cloths? Were they patterns or models for future textiles? The repetition of identical figures in rows does not support this interpretation, when one or two would suffice for a pattern. And the embroidery is too irregular and sketchy to illustrate the effects of using different colours. We are left with the assumption that the needlework sets out in abbreviated form the significant motifs of larger textiles. The subjects found on more finished weaving, embroidery and likewise vase painting are here reduced to ideograms. One could almost speak of the needlework as 'writing'.

At all events the important fact is that these cloths derive from the Nazca culture, as shown by the humming-birds which appear both on them and on Nazca bowls; but the same motif also appears in post-Nazca Morro graves. It is thus once again probable that early Nazca culture persisted despite the incursion of the Morro culture (or possibly that the shaft-graves of the Morro culture are older than has been thought).

The Berlin Museum für Völkerkunde has several small cloths 'in the Paracas style' with figures sketched on in needlework (Eisleb, vol. XI., fig. 12). Junius B. Bird has remarked on the necessity to publish the small number of similar samplers in public and private museums (Bennett and Bird, 1960 ed., p. 293).

The larger of the two embroidered cloths provides a connection with another embroidered textile from an *unusual early Nazca grave* which I excavated in 1932 near *188* Cahuachi. The body lay on its side wrapped in a gauze ▲ cloth and was first thought to be that of a child. Closer examination showed it in fact to be the contracted figure of a full-grown man who had been beheaded. His turban of red cord was wound not round a head but round the top of the vertebral column; a cloth had been draped over it to give the appearance of a head. The grave shows how important magical symbolism was to the ancients: the *beheaded man was equipped with a fine, embroidered cloth* *188* as well as with a red turban and a reddish-blue cloth for the ▼ face. One of the finest *jars with humming-bird decoration* *189* was held to be appropriate to this burial. The dead man must have been a significant person, otherwise his grave would not have been so distinguished. The head may have been lost as a trophy, but his body was still endowed with magical power.

The two-headed beast on the embroidered cloth *(188, below)* provides a link between this and the patterned cloth illustrated in pl. *186*, where there are five similar fabulous figures in a row stitched on the left half near the bottom edge. The embroidery on the beheaded man's magical cloth also relates to many other examples, as well as to three-dimensional needlework from the Paracas necropolis, in the southern style which is richest in textiles and either contemporary with the (early) Nazca or its successor, thus providing further evidence for the relative chronological framework of the early cultures of the south.

The famous Paracas tapestry in the Göteborg Museum was also from the grave of a beheaded man (d'Harcourt, 1948, p. 241).

190 *Fragment of a basket or 'snail' seat made from bound and coiled plant stems*, such as we often encountered in 1932 walking over the desert *pampa* of Las Trancas. They were an unfailing index of *caracol* (snail) graves, and one soon came upon the usual associated decorated sherds, textiles with corner brocading, remnants of shrouds and even trophy heads.

Trophy heads are equally usual as a *Leitfossil* of this important basket-grave culture, which lies between the early

191 Nazca and Coast Tiahuanaco. *Two trophy heads in situ in a grave on the ranch near Cahuachi*, showing bundles of red string over the eyes and a hole in the brow by which the head could be hung.

There must have been an intense belief in the efficacy of trophy heads. They were repeatedly painted on Nazca burial pottery and modelled in clay. Trophy heads were often captured; they were needed above all as a charm for a rich harvest. There were two lying over heads of maize in grave I at Cahuachi, at the feet of the dead man and turned towards him *(179)*.

Trophy heads disappear at the end of the Tiahuanaco culture and human sacrifices are found *(176)* in their place. The late *Algodón* graves (with mummies wrapped in cotton cloth) of the last centuries before the Spanish conquest had neither. In these the dead were placed, sitting or kneeling, not towards the south but towards the east, a fundamental change alongside which the practice of head deformation also disappeared.

A *head without deformation* found covered by the sand of 192 Copara.

165

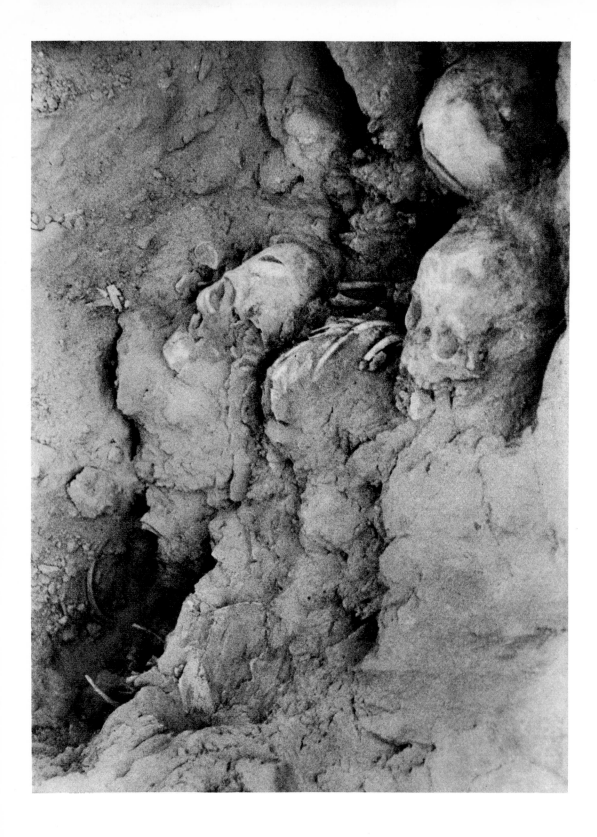

181

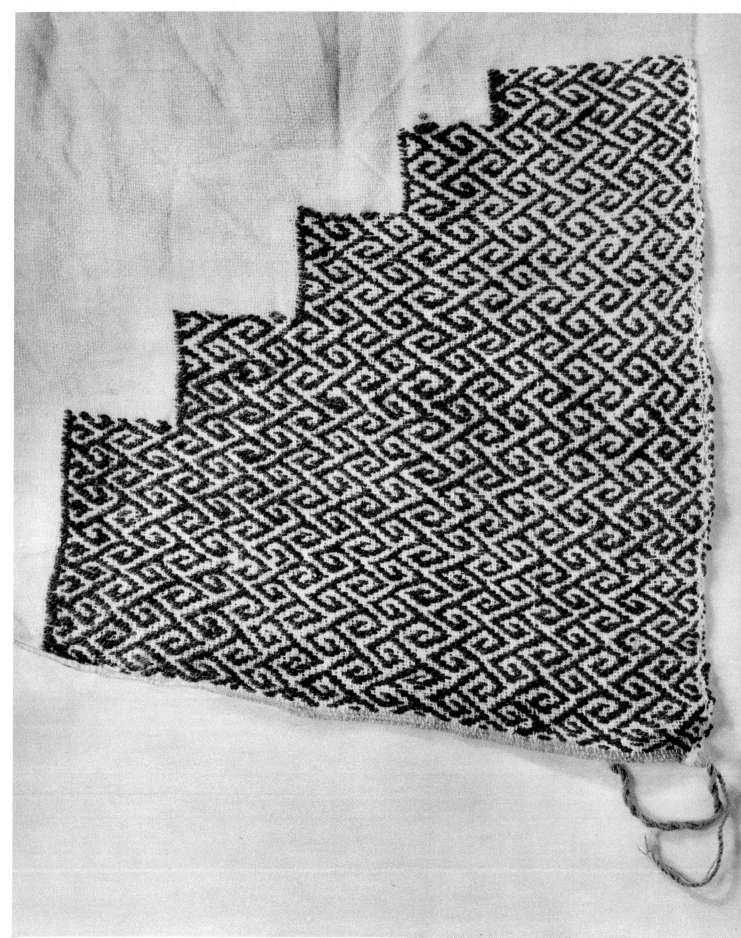

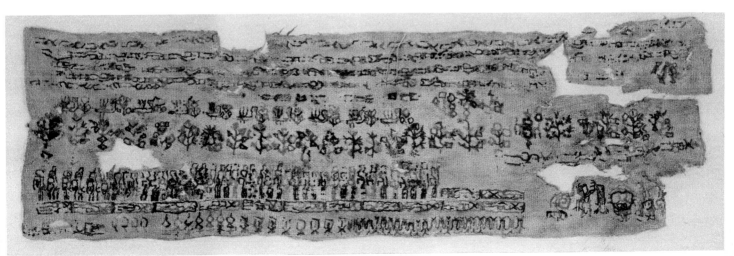

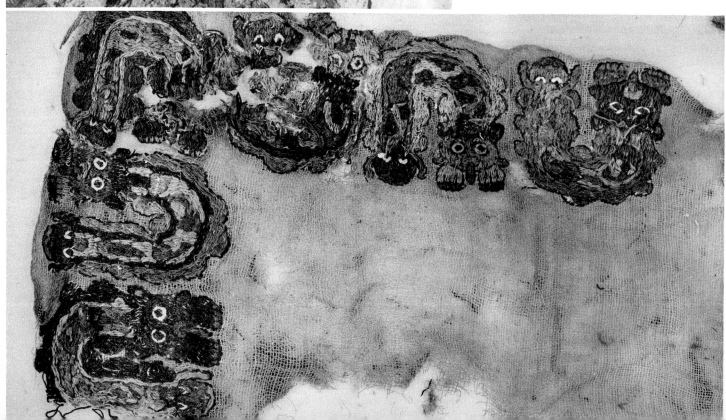

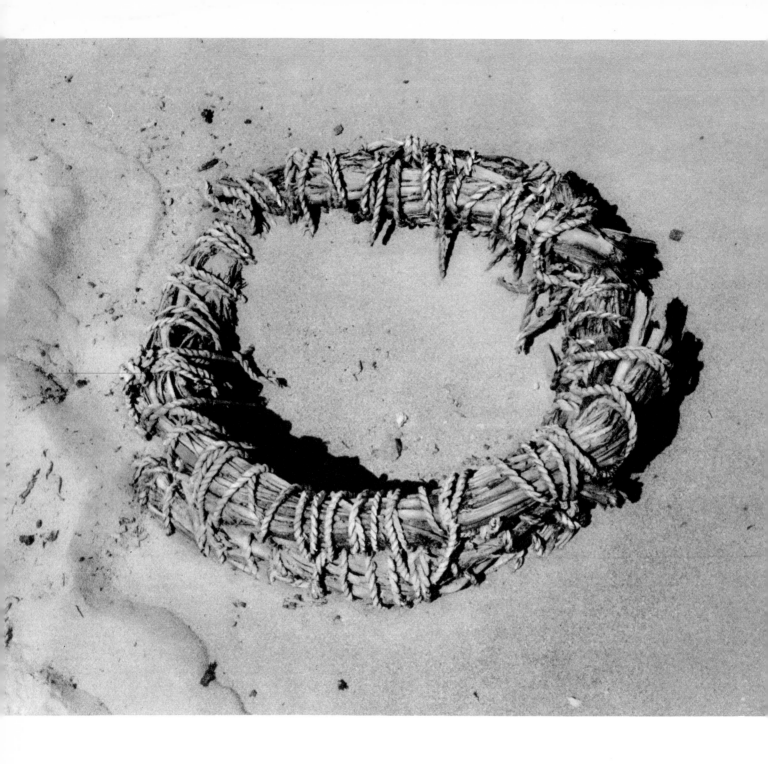

PACHECO

201 *An urn from Pacheco* in the Nazca valley in southern Peru, representing a human figure though with only the head and hands in detail. The body is formed by the vessel itself and is shown wrapped in a mantle painted in Coast Tiahuanaco style. Especially striking is the pattern of the painting on the face, which occurs on other Pacheco heads (for example in the Gaffron Collection in the Chicago Art Institute). There also exist heads of equal size without face painting. Most of these easily broken vessels (which include masterly models of llamas) come from one find-spot under a huge spreading huarango tree. Sherds were first found there by treasure-seekers at the beginning of the century and later Dr Tello discovered many outstanding pieces. It is noteworthy that almost all the urns lay broken in the soil as though they had been smashed in a struggle. None of them, however, came from a grave deposit.

Among the problems which arise from the Pacheco finds is their unmistakable stylistic connection with older – and remote – cultures of the north, such as the Mochica culture. But there is also a connection with the products, especially the textiles, of earlier cultures in the south, in particular the Nazca culture (Doering, 1927). And finally there are the considerations of physical anthropology. The strong and clear-cut features depicted at Pacheco are still found today among the Aymará who live in the southern Andes around Lake Titicaca. The French Créqui-Montfort expedition photographed young Aymará whose features closely resembled the Pacheco heads. There is no doubt that the site is an indication of the arrival of mountain people on the coast, who were at first dominated by the coastal tribes. We encountered related people, who had also come down from the mountains, in the Coast Tiahuanaco graves at Locarí *(172–177)*. The Locarí people, however, maintained themselves as lords of the land, as their tomb sacrifices show *(176)*.

SOUTHERN ANDES

Landscape

The remaining sections of this book are devoted to southern Andean country, which was the homeland of the Inca and their culture. The journey there takes us past the town of Arequipa at an altitude of 7,000 ft., lying like a flat bowl at the foot of a volcano.

202 This is the *Misti volcano* (18,500 ft.); its classical conical outline compares with Mt Fuji in Japan, Popocatepetl in Mexico and Osorno in Chile. It rises above a landscape cultivated since ancient times. Near Paucarpata the peasants dig and harvest on terraces which were already established under Inca rule. They lie around the base of the volcano like huge temple steps and fill the landscape with their horizontal lines.

To reach Cuzco, the sacred city of the Inca, we must climb to a great height to the cold and lonely high steppe of Puna, with its shy gazelle-like vicuñas.

203 The *salt lake* (or *Salinas;* 14,450 ft.), still in sight of Misti, with Chachani rising on the right. Indian shepherds guard their llama herds on its banks. On the far side of the lake can be seen an eddying column of salt dust.

The road continues through open, lonely country into the centre of the Inca realm, the sculptured landscape of Cuzco. The mountains are cut to sharper outlines by the headwaters of the large rivers which rush down towards the Amazon. Snow-covered mountain peaks alternate with plateaux and high valleys called *Quechua*, after which the language of the inhabitants is named. The sky looks tempestuous above the open, treeless highlands. Single bright storm clouds almost dazzle one and intensify the deep blue of the sky. It is *a wonderful land,* especially in the 204 spring when shadows of the clouds are blown across the green of the plains. The plants in the foreground are cotton-grass.

The *18-ft. stem of an agave,* its buds like beaten bronze, 205 thrusting up against the endless bright sky with white clouds blown from the east. This alpine terrain ends where the *sub-tropical mountain woodland* begins. Moist winds 206 blowing in from the east across the Hylaea, the great tree mass of the Amazon, release heavy rainfall when they rise over the opposing flank of the Cordilleras, and so bring about the forest zone of the *montaña*. This photograph was taken near Tres Curces (over 12,500 ft. above sea-level), east of Cuzco, showing the last outlying trees of the rain belt with the treeless highlands, the home of the Quechua, in bright sunshine beyond.

The Quechua live in the high valleys and on *wide plains* 207 *between the snow-peaks* at a height of from 9,000 to 12,000 ft., in villages and on single farms, tending their fields and endlessly crossing the mountains along high tracks.

INCA ROADS

Cuzco region

In the Cuzco highlands we again encounter the remains of 208 the great Inca roads. This is the *calzada de Lucre*, an embanked road across swampland. Parts of the side-walls are still standing. This is a link-road and on the far side of the 209 valley bottom it joins the *calzada de Muyna*, part of the *camino real de la sierra*, the royal highway of the mountains. Its walled embankment *(calzada)* still stands clear to a height of 6 ft. and carries the road over the lakeland near Muyna (a ruined Inca city). For four hundred years traffic from Cuzco to the south to Lake Titicaca has followed this highway. Not only did the Inca legions pass over it en route for their stations in far-off Chile; it is still used today by heavy lorries and buses.

A third embanked road, the *calzada de Anta*, crossing 210 the *swampy Pampa de Anta*, seen at ground-level and 211 from the air (north-west of Cuzco). The royal mountain highway was laid straight across the plain on an embankment 6 miles long, 22 ft. wide and 3 ft. high. It is probable that this embankment also had flanking walls which have gradually been covered over. After four hundred years the road is still used throughout its length.

PEASANTS OF THE HIGHLANDS

Cuzco region

The descendants of the road-builders, the Quechua, are still numerous in the high valleys of the same name. *Rupuerto Aurecosy of Llanacuna* (Chincheros) is a Quechua. Among the mountain peasants various forms are found in the heads of individuals, as can be seen by comparing this inhabitant of Chincheros with the man from Quiquijana in the Huilcanota valley *(214)*. The blood of the Inca peasantry still runs in the tribes *(ayllus)* of the highland villages, the former Quechua who were the principal representatives of the Inca empire. Quechua was the official language from the southern border of present-day Colombia to southern Chile.

The crystal clearness of the air at over 9,000 ft. is shown in this *landscape near Chincheros*. The slopes and peaks of the mountains some 25 miles away can be seen almost as clearly as the Indian woman on the path rising on the far side of the lake.

Decoration of the woollen cloak or *poncho* in the Cuzco region is very varied. Every day many Quechua Indians travel into the town of Cuzco and it is possible to recognize from their ponchos which part of the Cuzco area they come from. *Valentino Huamán from Quiquijana* in the Huilcanota valley has a *kenko* pattern on his poncho: 'the sinuous one', as the sacred rocks in the Sacsayhuaman region are also called, after the zig-zag channel for offerings *(247)*. The principal colour of the cloak is red. Huamán is thirty-two years old, and about 5 ft. 6 in. tall; in appearance he is typical of the mountain peasants of the Cuzco region: slender and muscular, with a bright cloak worn over Spanish colonial dress with its knee breeches, and a flat hat of woven straw covered with bright wool, over a knitted woollen cap. Leather sandals are worn on the feet. There are many such individuals in the southern highlands, typical of the region of the Quechua.

Among the Indians of the Huilcanota valley above Cuzco one encounters a narrow-faced type with a finely drawn profile and often a strikingly well-proportioned nose, like this young *Quechua from Pitumarca*. This is the type of face seen in the famous Mochica portrait head *(158, 159)*; however the portrait is almost fifteen hundred years old, and comes from the north coast over 600 miles from the valleys of the southern Andes. We can only remark on the likeness.

Men of Inca times might be personified in the *Quechua Eusebio Choque from Andamarca*, near Lauramarca, a powerful, representative figure about 5 ft. 7 in. tall.

He rarely spoke and never laughed. He is seen wearing a splendid cloak with dark-red and blue ornamentation on a light-red ground. The diamond shapes in the stripes of the pattern were explained to me as 'gardens with flowers' on other similar cloaks, and the four bordering stripes as 'flutes'. I should have liked to buy the poncho and offered a good price. Choque's response, 'no', was the sole word he addressed to me.

It seemed to me that the faces of the Indians became proportionately more delicate as we approached the forest on the eastern limit of the Andes. The *young peasant from Capana* in the Paucartambo valley, holding a llama on a black and white woollen cord, was less than 5 ft. 3 in. in height, an entirely unprejudiced man, cheerful and friendly, and not in the least shy of the camera although he had never left his remote mountain valleys.

Celestino Huancca from Sumana in the Paucartambo valley was born in the same remote regions of the eastern Andes. Reserved and taciturn, he kept his face from us; even in his working clothes he was a striking figure. In the background of his native valley stood Apu Ausangate (20,500 ft.), one of the mightiest snow-peaks of the Cordilleras, a 'father of the torrent'. *Apu* means 'master', a title the highland people confer on every high mountain which they revere as a god.

CUZCO

Architecture and sacred cliffs

The inhabitants of Cuzco are surrounded by the works of their ancestors. Antiquity is everywhere in evidence. Its remains are like the lines of an ancient script. Walking through Cuzco at night the hand often brushes against the cool dark stones of a royal residence or a temple of Inca times.

220 The *main temple in Cuzco, the 'Coricancha'* or golden court, was dedicated to the country's principal god, the sun god. It also contained the temple rooms of the moon goddess, the thunder god, the planet Venus, of the stars and the rainbow. The ancient Andean people's masterly stonework can be admired in the remains of the Coricancha, which are today partially hidden under the church and monastery of Santo Domingo. The *stones of the exposed 'apse'* must have been adapted to the curvature and inclination of the wall. At the same time the ground-plan of the 'apse' is not in the form of an ellipse, but an irregular curve *(220)*. The curvature is greatest on the left. In this it resembles the line of the tower surrounding the sacrificial cliffs in Machu Picchu *(294)*. The sun temple was the most sacred and the richest in the Inca empire. Its discoverers record wide wall friezes in gold leaf, and we must keep these in mind in trying to imagine the original appearance of the temple. The mummies of dead Inca rulers were seated in the temple hall of the sun god, among them Huayna Capac, the last of the great Inca, placed alone opposite the picture of the sun. The son of Tupac Yupanqui, also named 'the great', and grandson of the still greater Pachacutec, he was the last of this line. Under Huayna Capac the Inca empire reached its widest extent, from the river Ancasmayu, the blue river, on the southern border of present-day Colombia, to the river Maule in southern Chile. After his death the empire broke up. His legitimate son Huascar was killed by his illegitimate son Atahualpa before he had time to establish himself. Atahualpa appears to have been a decadent ruler, if the dominant traits ascribed to him in the reports of the Spanish chroniclers are not misleading.

Already several years before his death Huayna Capac had apparently received news of strange seafarers, the Spaniards on their exploratory expeditions towards the south, and seems to have been anxious about the future. He died before the onslaughts he feared took place. He might possibly have withstood them better than did Atahualpa, although he himself may not have been able to prevent the incipient breakdown of the empire, which had begun before the Spaniards arrived.

One of the *most ingenious sculptures in the Coricancha* is 222 found in the outer wall of the so-called temple of the planet Venus. Half-hidden by a colonial-period door pillar can be seen the fragment of a wall with niches, with a sculptured slab, partially broken off, jutting forward. There are regular channels and holes worked on its surface, apparently for stone or metal inlay. Garcilasso tells of twelve 'tabernacles' in the temple walls around the inner court, faced with gold; indeed, it reads as though Garcilasso meant the entire niches were lined with gold. Precious stones (turquoise) were set along the edges and in the corners. During festivals in honour of the sun god the Inca is reported to have sat in one of the tabernacles, which would be chosen in accordance with the season of the year.

Garcilasso's description fits exactly with the remains of the niche in our illustration. The niche opens towards the east (or east-north-east). It could therefore be a remnant of one of the gleaming thrones set with gold and precious stones from which the ruling Inca (the *Sapay Inca*) participated in the sun rites.

One of the basic features of Inca architecture at Cuzco, the *trapezoidal niche*, built in its classical form, is seen here 223 in the temple room of the stars in the Coricancha: height 2 ft. 8 in., width 17 in. below and 14½ in. above, depth 15 in.

Garcilasso's description is apparently reliable and allows us to imagine how sumptuous and colourful the temple must have been with its full furnishings. The bare monumental walls are impressive today in their structure and technical accomplishment. Beside the wealth of their former inlay and hangings we must conjure up a picture of the rich and symbolic costumes of the worshippers, like those we have seen from graves on the southern Peruvian coastlands. Only then do the ruins come to life, alike in this and other temples, and in palaces and royal courts near or far from Cuzco.

The royal courts whose walls still stand in the streets of Cuzco are variously constructed. Some are truly defensive, with walls of polygonal, cushion-shaped blocks set, despite their size, with tight joints effected by grinding *(224, below)*. The projections on the lower surface of many of the blocks may have served primarily in the positioning of the tree-levers when they were transported. The massive wall in our picture belongs to the *royal court of the Inca* 224 *Roca*. In the lists of rulers of Sarmiento de Gamboa and of Garcilasso de la Vega (whose mother was an Inca princess, so that he added 'the Inca' to his name) Roca is the sixth ruler. To Inca Roca is attributed by tradition the founding of the school of learned men, the *amauta*.

225 Later royal courts, like the *Pucumarca, or red tower* of the Inca Tupac Yupanqui, are characterized by long regular courses of ashlar masonry. The stones have slightly convex faces and are cut to fit tightly together without mortar.

SACSAYHUAMAN

226 *The Sacsayhuaman,* which is often called a fortress, stands above the old royal city of Cuzco on a promontory jutting out from the flanking hills into the Huatanay valley. According to tradition the Inca Pachacutec laid the plans for this enormous work; the construction was begun by his son Tupac Yupanqui and completed by his grandson Huayna Capac. According to this account it would have been built in the course of the fifteenth century AD. But there can be no doubt that parts of the Sacsayhuaman are much older, especially the lowest and strongest of the three zig-zag walls (fig. 7 and *228, 229*). In the photograph these lie on the left, on the side of the promontory away from the town, where it is joined to the surrounding hills by a flat ridge.

227 A *head of an Inca in stone* dating from the years before or after the fall of the Inca empire in the first half of the sixteenth century. At the side of the head is one of the characteristic large decorative discs which were attached to the ears. Over the brow hangs the *borla del Inca (mascapaycha* in Quechua), the red fringe or tassel which was the Inca 'crown'. The head was reported found near the Kenko cliff (*247*). It appears originally to have been covered with white stucco; whether this was painted on can no longer be established.

While the two upper zig-zag walls of the Sacsayhuaman are reminiscent of the dimensions of the royal court of the Inca (*224*), the *lowest wall of the citadel* is a gigantic work of overwhelming and monumental proportions. The corner block shown in pl. *229* is 16 ft. high. The *great cubic monolith* (right, foreground) by the gateway is 10 ft. 6 in. high, 9 ft. 6 in. wide and 6 ft. 9 in. thick. Above this lowest and earliest wall run two other zig-zag walls (fig. 7). A *high gate with the trapezoidal outline of Inca architecture* opens through the middle wall: 11 ft. 6 in. high, 5 ft. wide below and 3 ft. 6 in. above; the lintel block is 8 ft. long, 3 ft. wide and 2 ft. 6 in. high.

The mortarless jointing of the great blocks of the Sacsayhuaman is no less precise than in the royal courts of the city. In looking at a *detail of the wall jointing* we can comprehend the wonder of those who visit the site; the photograph shows a section of the wall about 9 ft. long. It is not possible to insert even a fine knife blade into the crack. All the blocks have an outward convexity of surface, like a low cushion. The mighty *corner stone* is shown here on its prepared horizontal base, like the foot of some gigantic elephant.

Garcilasso records further building on the summit of the Sacsayhuaman inside the walls, including three towers. The base-walls of such buildings have been discovered by the Cuzco Archaeological Institute under the direction

228, 229
230
231
232
233

of Dr Luis E. Valcarel. The zig-zag line of the walls has been put forward as proof that the Sacsayhuaman was a defensive work, designed as protection against an attack from the flank. I cannot myself follow this interpretation, which is based on the weapons and fighting methods proper to far-off Europe. What decisively dismisses the thesis that this was a fortification is the fact that other encircling or boundary walls in the Cuzco region, which were certainly not defensive, were also laid in a zig-zag line. I have seen zig-zag walls in the cliff labyrinth of Lanlacuyoc on the heights behind the Sacsayhuaman, at a little sanctuary near the Kenko, as well as near the remarkable Quillarumi stone *(263)* west of the Pampa de Anta, and near Pumamarca, a deserted building near the road from Cuzco to Chitapampa. Although we do not understand its meaning, zig-zag construction was in some way related to those buildings, cliffs and caves which were held sacred. Zig-zag walls were not defensive, as is clear from those built around stones; their significance derives from the features which they surround. I believe it must have been likewise with the Sacsayhuaman. The nucleus of the monument must have been a sanctuary, perhaps a shrine like those so often encountered in the highlands. It could originally have been the shrine of the king's clan. Garcilasso states explicitly that the Sacsayhuaman was 'also a house of the sun'. From the outset such a sanctuary would be defended, as such sites are on the highlands (cf. the 'stronghold' of Ollantaytambo, pls *269* ff.); but in their purpose and form these are not primarily defensive structures.

On the plateau behind the Sacsayhuaman are numerous examples of remarkable worked stones and rock groups. To walk over this windy terrain is to encounter simple niches, steps, large and small altars, throne-like seats and groupings of various geometric figures, which in the past had meaning and purpose. It is almost like a simple lapidary script cut on a large scale in the living rock.

234,235 One of the best known of these stone sculptures is the so-called *throne of the Inca on the Suchuna rocks* opposite the Sacsayhuaman. It consists of a series of steps cut in the rock, with a total width of nearly 40 ft. The Inca is said to have sat there to watch ceremonies on the little plain between Suchana and the Sacsayhuaman. This is an open question. The steps do not face the plain, but are oriented due east, a plan which is more readily related to sun festivals. The striking precision in the angles and surfaces of the steps, too, seems to have been dictated less by artistic considerations than by requirements which we can only suppose

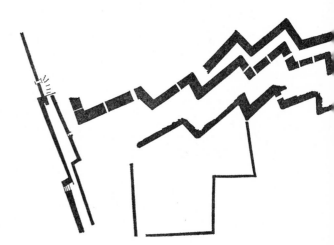

were those of astronomy, serving in this instance a religious purpose.

There are three steps to the north and a flight of nine to the south of the central platform, which measures 6 ft. by 2 ft. 8 in. The twelve steps – the number may have reference to the months of the year – are of approximately the same dimensions: 2 ft. 9 in. wide (one exception being 2 ft. 7 in.) and 2 ft. 10 in. deep. A second line of shallower steps has been cut alongside below the main series, the front edges somewhat irregular and running into the rock. In front again are a pair of wide steps, 7 ft. 6 in. wide by 4 ft. 9 in.

In the hilly country between the Sacsayhuaman and the mountains lie the *ruins of the Tampu Machay* (the 'cave of *236,237* the inn'), though this name seems rather to relate to an actual cave which lies above the ruins. Tradition connects

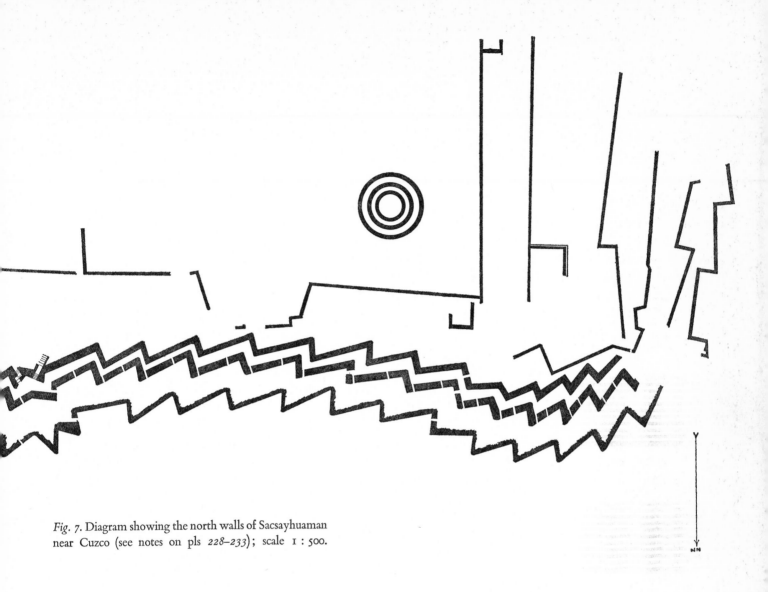

Fig. 7. Diagram showing the north walls of Sacsayhuaman near Cuzco (see notes on pls *228–233*); scale 1 : 500.

the remains of the buildings with Tupac Yupanqui, as a country seat of the Inca; but interpretation of them as a little temple seems preferable. The 'soul' of the site is concealed, on the left, in a spring which has been led into a stone channel, to fall over the walled terraces, its sound breaking the silence of the little valley. It is one of the most charming spots in the Cuzco region. Taken together the stepped terraces rise to a height of 30 ft. Alongside regular masonry with large stones in horizontal courses, and with four large door-like niches in the highest wall, one finds polygonal stone-work with boulders set in a pattern resembling a honey-comb. Similar work occurs in late extensions at the Roca palace in Cuzco; it was a technique which survived for a considerable time.

Among the forms carved into the rocks on the plateau
238 behind the Sacsayhuaman are *throne-like seats or altars,*

invariably made up of three parts: a central section, which stands out by the manner in which it is cut, and two side sections. This threefold division of the thrones or altars in the open air seems to have been designed for a definite cult, as we meet it again in the region around Cuzco. The carved rock *Chingana Grande* (the great labyrinth) 239 a short distance below Suchana is covered with a profusion of carvings, and contains a three-part throne or altar in a central position. The Chingana stone is 18 ft. high and the legend of the 'weary stone' seems to relate to it: Garcilasso tells how a colossal rock, dragged by twenty thousand workers, broke loose while being transported to the Sacsayhuaman and killed three thousand in its fall. The Chingana stone, however, was certainly never intended for the Sacsayhuaman; nor has it ever been moved from its present position. It is covered with flights of steps, with seats and altars, many of which appear to overlap, like a model in which every corner has significance, fashioned in the belief that the whole stone is one magical complex. The largest carving on the Chingana stone is the throne or altar in three sections, 10 ft. high and surrounded by single steps of different heights. The two most prominent of the carved rock outcrops on the highlands above Cuzco and both still within the Sacsayhuaman's sphere of influence

240 are *Kenko* and *Lacco* (also called *Kenko grande*). The *Kenko is a riven mass of outcrop* cut through with natural faults and

241 cavities. To the north-east of it lies a *level arena for festivals* and cult celebrations, enclosed by the wide curve of a *wall with niches*, from which the covering stones have disappeared.

Near the focal point of the wall's curve, on a rectangular

243 walled pedestal, stands the *jaguar monument,* a natural rock 15 ft. high, which is regarded as portraying a seated jaguar. On its pedestal of carefully hewn ashlar blocks it looks like a great statue. Like the arena and the niched wall it was uncovered during the excavations by the Cuzco Archaeological Institute. The stone is a monument of the very ancient South American statue cult in the region of the Andes.

244 The heart of the Kenko is enclosed in a *cave entered between overhanging and smooth-hewn walls,* a gateway to the underworld. Inside the cave we are in the realm of the dead. Altar-like pedestals and tables are carved into the walls. A large *throne or altar* in three sections towering 6 ft. high 245 stands out from the rocks, with a low back wall. A deep cleft behind it recedes into subterranean realms. Perhaps it was the seat of a mummy during ancestral celebrations, like the many other stone seats in the open air about Cuzco. In the beliefs of the Andean people man arises from the earth and returns to it in death.

The *surface of the Kenko*, like that of the Chingana Grande 246 stone, is covered with carvings: step-like overlapping plat-forms, seats (*240*), altars and channels for offerings; and we know almost nothing of the significance either of the parts or the whole of this complex.

A *channel for offerings* cut in a zig-zag through the rock 247 like the writhing body of a snake, is called the *Kenko* – the sinuous one – and has given its name to the whole rock. It runs down from a basin for offerings (in the right half of the photograph rather above the centre) and conveys the drink-offering down into the underworld. It resembles the ground-plan of the zig-zag wall of the Sacsayhuaman (fig. 7).

The *natural Kenko outcrop is set in walls* of very evenly cut 248 ashlar blocks in order to emphasize the sanctity of the natural shrine.

continued on p. 249

257 The *Lacco* (Kenko Grande) also conveys us into the mysteries of the realm of the dead. It is a more massive outcrop, towering up higher than the Kenko, more remote and farther from the Sacsayhuaman.

The flower-covered Lacco is divided into two by a deep cleft. A group of carvings can be seen on the left framing 258 the entrance to *cave I*. Among them are steep and narrow ladder-like steps rising up from ground-level; these are footings for walls which were designed either to divide little cult rooms or simply to enclose the entrance, like a door into the shrine. Similar footings occur in the Inca-misana rocks *(281)*.

259 *Over the entrance to cave I* a slab of rock is jammed suspend-▼ ed like a giant thunderbolt. Inside in the twilight there are several flat wall niches to the left which could have held statues of gods. The cave curves round to the right and narrows into a cleft which disappears into the earth. If we follow along the face of the Lacco rock to the right we 259 reach, almost at the end, an *unusual flight of steps*, not ▲ arranged for a direct ascent but forcing the climber from side to side. We have not found out its magical name. Half-way up this flight of steps we find the *entrance to* 260 *cave II of the Lacco* which is more elaborately carved than that of cave I. On the smooth stone wall on the right a snake carved in relief writhes towards the cave's interior *(260, above)*. Turning round in the cave one sees massive entrance pillars cut out of the rock, with a form of shallow steps leading out into the open air *(260, below)*. Near the steps to the right are carved two pumas which crouch facing the light. We cannot be certain whether these animals symbolize the emergence of mankind from the bowels of the earth, and the snake man's return into the inner darkness. Where the cave terminates in almost total 261 darkness an *altar-shaped seat* rises up, about 6 ft. wide and 5 ft. deep: the ceremonial throne of the dead, abandoned among the silence of the rocks. Here we are in the presence of the subterranean powers who emerge from the rock clefts near the throne and disappear back into them. Ancestors had the power of good and evil, and to honour the dead and invoke their benevolence was a fundamental requirement. The carved rocks around the Sacsayhuaman, of which we have illustrated only several of the most important examples, were ceremonial sites from which noble and royal clans derived their being. I believe the Sacsayhuaman itself to be, in essence, a sanctuary of the royal tribe of the Inca.

Travelling north-west from Cuzco over the Arcopunco pass onto the high plateau of Anta and then down again to the right along the deep Huaracondo ravine one reaches the Urubamba valley. In the left-hand wall of the ravine is one of the most wonderful of the Inca sanctuaries, the cave of *Choquequilla,* the Golden Moon, with an ingenious 262 carving on the rock in front of the entrance. Even for the ▲ highly developed lapidary art of the southern Andes this is an extraordinary work. The central stepped symbol recalls a similar motif on the 'bath of the princess' near Ollantaytambo *(283)*. But at neither site can we be sure of its significance. Unfortunately, treasure-seekers have tried to blow up the monument, although no treasure could possibly be expected inside the natural rock into which it is cut. In the centre above the ancient sacred stepped symbol we can still see where the charge was laid to blast off the whole upper portion.

The *interior of the Golden Moon cave* is dominated by a flat 262 niche about 15 ft. wide, with a further niche 4 ft. wide ▼ sunk into its back wall. Right across the whole niche runs a black stripe, an inch or two broad, like that on a wall in the Cuzco sun temple. The stone in front of the Golden Moon cave, the Concacha valley stone *(267)*, and the Moon stone *(263)* are among the masterpieces of ancient American stone carving, and we shall return to them.

The road rises again onto the Pampa de Anta, which is crossed on the old Inca road *(210, 211)*, and ascends to a pass. Before reaching it there is an upland moor to the right, covered with boulders. Near a settlement of Indian peasants almost 12,000 ft. above sea-level is a little, damp gorge, ringed round by high grey cliffs. There is a spring, and rows of ancient altar stones can be distinguished. A few paces above the spring one catches sight of the *Quillarumi,* the Moon Stone: a semi-circle 8 ft. across, 263 chiselled and ground on a convenient natural rock face. Its surface is as smooth as marble in contrast to the natural weathered stone surrounding it. All the angles are cut as though with precision instruments and the contrast be-tween the clean lines and the perfect curve and the rough unworked rock covered with lichen lends additional charm to the sculpture. What is the significance of the stone? The key to its secret may well lie in the seven flat steps traversing the perfectly proportioned curve, which faces exactly to the east. Three narrower steps run down on either side of the wider central one. Without doubt it is not the actual surface of the steps which is the deter-mining factor, but the setting of their edges. The im-pression that this is an observatory can scarcely be avoided by anyone who views the carving. There is an unmistakable similarity to the Suchana rock *(234, 235)*, which was also oriented eastwards. Despite the name 'Moon Stone', which derives rather from the outline of the monument, we must think above all of the sun (which in the mountains is far more prominent than the moon) as the body whose movements are relevant to this stone.

The Concacha stones, which were our next goal, lie on the far side of the Apurimac on the heights near Abancay. The road leads over the high pass (*c.* 12,000 ft.) of Casacancha (or Huillcaconga, according to Middendorf) to descend into the broad gorge of the Apurimac river (the 'talkative one'), which it crosses by a modern suspension bridge at 4,500 ft. above sea-level, and then winds upwords to the pass called in Quechua '*Where the Inca blows his flute*'.

The silence is broken only by the sighing of the wind, the cry of a shepherd or by thunder. Beyond these *undulating heights soars a line of high peaks* reaching heights of over 15,000 ft.; on the right is the snow-covered Salcantay mountain, and on the left Choquequiraú with its great glaciers and a powdering of white on the crags. On these heights lie the *Concacha stones*. They are also called the Saihuite stones, since they are on a farm of that name. I use the first name which has become established in the literature. There are three stones and one can be seen rather to the left of the centre of the photograph, lying like a great bright egg on the hillside. I call this the Hill Stone *(266)*. The other two stones lie on the valley bottom behind the hill and can be called the Valley Stones *(267)*. On the upper edge of the slope in pl. *265* the remains of a supporting wall of squared stones can still be distinguished. It seems as though the slope was originally terraced and would have had the appearance of a flat stepped pyramid, in an attempt to achieve even here the dominant form of religious monument in ancient Peru. The *Hill Stone at Concacha* is an ovoid monolith, 13 ft. 6 in. long, 10 ft. wide and 8 ft. 6 in. high. Numerous figures have been carved into its upper half, some in high relief, some almost free-standing, though still attached to the natural stone. They include human figures, pumas, llamas, vicuñas, monkeys, lizards, frogs, crabs and snakes, as well as meandering irrigation canals and little temples with steps and niches in between. Winding through this world of figures are flat grooves an inch or two wide. They all originate in a dish at the stone's highest point and run down with many ramifications to end at the lower edge of the sculptured mound, discharging through round holes. The course of an offering poured into the dish as it made its way down through the figures might serve as an augury. We do not understand the meaning of the individual figures. They might signify gods or demons and perhaps stars. The different sizes of the figures should not be overlooked since they are not rendered in proportion. The men are very small; powerful pumas and large apes cower nearby and a gigantic snake winds around. The treatment of the little temple models is masterly. The stone is no longer in its original position. It has been tilted towards the north by people digging for treasure underneath. An offering cannot flow through all the channels the mason provided to receive it. Some of the figures are so damaged that they cannot be identified, all of which complicates interpretation of the stone's significance. The damage seems to be old since the surface of the broken parts is as weathered as the rest.

Over the brow of the hill is a valley which runs down towards the Apurimac. The two other Concacha stones, the Valley Stones, lie in the hollow and their planes and steps can already be distinguished from above. The path to them descends steeply, crossing meadows and streams, to reach the smaller stone standing in front of the larger. The *larger Valley Stone at Concacha* (20 ft. wide) is fascinating and looks more like the work of the gods than of men. The Valley Stones are not carved with figures. The stone has been treated geometrically, like the monuments of the Sacsayhuaman region, with steps and broad altar surfaces; on one side there are supporting vertical features. A group of seven small dishes has been worked on the level upper surface of the block, and from an eighth dish near the edge a deep groove leads to the wall of the stone, where it divides into two channels which terminate in obliquely lying offering-dishes. From these the drink-offering would have run down the wall. The whole block must have been split by lightning. However different it is from the Hill Stone, the dishes and channels have been laid out similarly at both sites. Nor can the Hill and Valley Stones be ascribed to different peoples or to different times. All three were worked in the same spirit. The Valley Stone belongs with the Kenko and Lacco stones and is of the same period and worked by the same or related people. Pumas and snakes occur in the Lacco context and the Cusilluyoc stone has the remains of sculptured animal figures similar to the Concacha Hill Stone. These sacred stones, and especially the Valley Stones, lie in an arcadian landscape, in the sunlight between wind-blown trees and the murmur and rippling of streams and springs.

268 *Ollantaytambo* achieves a greatness never repeated in ancient Peru. It is impossible to say which is more admirable, the line of the curved terraces *(269)*, the granite facing of the temple front *(274, 275)*, the wonderful finish of the stones *(271, 277)*, the exact form of the polygonal blocks *(272, 273)*, the beauty of the valley or the position of the citadel on a steep mountain spur *(268)* between the Urubamba and Patacancha valleys, and visible from a great distance. The work of man and nature fall into perfect harmony.

Ollantaytambo, or more properly Ollantaytampu, was called simply *tampu* by the chronicler Garcilasso, which meant 'royal court' or 'camp' in Inca times. Ollantay is the name of a contemporary general; there is a play in the Quechua language about his love for a princess of the Inca Pachacutec's line. Ollantaytambo is called a citadel, as is the Sacsayhuaman. However, even less than Sacsayhuaman is it a defensive work, but rather a temple city. The entrails of the dead Inca were buried in the temple at Ollantaytambo, while the mummies of the kings were assembled round the image of the sun god in the sun temple at Cuzco.

Ollantaytambo must have had a great significance for the Inca, to have become the shrine for the entrails as well as the hearts of their dead kings. It must have stood in a special relationship to the Inca people and their royal houses, which must have related to their origins. This is not the only secret of Ollantaytambo. The main building, the centre of the temple city, lies near the left-hand edge of the photograph in pl. *268,* above the massive supply wall which supported the approach road for the mono-liths. One sees the mound of the temple and its long bright side wall turning sharply (on the right) to the front wall, which looks narrow and shaded in this view from the valley. There stand the great monoliths, the glory of Tampu *(274, 275)*. From the top of the temple mound a veritable cascade of walls runs down to the Patacancha river, like a great waterfall petrified into crystal. We see again the fundamental concepts of ancient American architecture: the fashioning of a sort of stepped pyramid by carving the high rocks of the hillside to form terraces, with the temple mound on the truncated summit.

269 The *facing walls of the terraces* follow the lines of the hillside and in places have concave curves. It is this feature which lends them charm, the feeling of movement. The *fine*
270 *gateway of the Inca* in the trapezoid style (or more precisely,

in the Cuzco-Inca style) in the upper north-west terrace is a typical product of the Inca architect. Behind the gate to the left is a *wall with niches* executed in granite; the preci- 271 sion of the workmanship is entrancing. The shield-shaped block is a mason's showpiece. We have encountered the angular insets on the upper sides of the stone at Cuzco in the court of the Inca Roca *(224, below)*. Following this wall almost to the end of the terrace we come to a passage leading to the left *flanked by four massive granite blocks.* 272 Despite their weight, the masonry has been set with the greatest precision. Under each was laid a narrower pedestal which abuts against a second base block, worked to receive the back corner of the principal granite blocks. Moreover the four blocks correspond almost exactly. The perfection of their form can be even better appreciated since they have been shifted out of their original positions, perhaps by an earthquake. The *adjacent flat blocks* do not match the 273 precision of the gate stones, although their mortarless joints are equally precise. The short projections on these and the previous blocks can most readily be explained as abutments for the positioning of levers during transport. On the *highest temple terrace at Ollantaytambo are six huge* 274 *monoliths* fronting the temple mound, which have given the site its fame. These monoliths, of light-red granite, are not convex in outline like the Sacsayhuaman megaliths but flat-faced with *isolated projections and a simple relief on* 275 *the fourth stone.* Narrow granite jointing-fillets have been inserted between the monoliths (a feature absent at the Sacsayhuaman), apparently to help secure the massive slabs. There is no use of mortar or other bonding. The uniqueness of this row of monoliths calls for data about their mass. Describing the stones from left to right *(274, above)*:

   I 11 ft. 3 in. high, 5 ft. 4 in. wide, 3 ft. 6 in. thick.
  II 11 ft. high, 5 ft. wide, 3 ft. 5 in. thick.
 III 12 ft. high, 4 ft. 10 in. wide, 2 ft. 3 in. thick.
  IV 11 ft. 6 in. high, 5 ft. 8 in. wide, 3 ft. thick.
   V 11 ft. 5 in. high, 6 ft. 6 in. wide above and
      6 ft. 10 in. below, 2 ft. 6 in. thick.
      The base is hidden and actual height is *c.* 12 ft.
  VI 13 ft. high, 6 ft. 3 in. wide above and 6 ft. 8 in.
      below, 5 ft. 7 in. thick above and 6 ft. 6 in. below.

It will be seen that the monoliths are not of equal thickness, and III, IV and V especially are reduced. These have consequently been walled behind by polygonal stones carefully fitted together, to approximate to the thickness of monoliths I and II. This has been done because the monolith wall is not laid directly against the rocks (of greenish schist) behind, but leaves a remarkable passage 3 ft. 6 in. to 4 ft. wide, about 25 ft. long and 6 ft. deep, which is closed by the side of the corner stone VI. The irregularities in the natural rock are partly filled in with simple dry-stone walling, and this walling has three small trapezoidal niches set close together. Thus when one climbs down into the passage there is a comparatively unimpressive wall, with three niches, and an imposing wall of finely worked stone. In this opposition lies one of the secrets of the construction of Ollantaytambo. We do not know what should be reconstructed on the foundation of the monoliths. A drawing by the painter Rugendas made in the 1840's (in the Munich Staatliche Graphische Sammlung) shows that they are not complete since he drew other stones, which it seems have since fallen and disappeared, lying *in situ* above them. In any case the temple was not completed. The prepared, or almost prepared, blocks of stone which are lying about on all sides are evidence of this, for they had never been erected. The section of the building in front of the monoliths is also unfinished *(274, below)*. Only the massive transom and its foundation are in position (17 ft. 6 in. long, 4 ft. 9 in. high and 3 ft. thick). After hundreds of years the edges are still straight and true. It cannot be overlooked that in the evenness of its surfaces and sharpness of its angles this structure differs from the wall of monoliths, which were unusual among other monolithic stones in the handling of these features. This is another puzzle posed by the architecture at Ollantaytambo.

276, 277 The charm of the stone *in the wall of monoliths* is difficult to describe. Its granular structure needs to be handled to be appreciated. The light-red of the granite resembles the colour of veal, with here and there a greenish or yellowish patination.

277 The *clear-cut stepped ornament on stone IV* is a fairly frequent symbol in ancient Peruvian art and must have reference to ascent and descent, to heaven and earth. The section of the monolith which is illustrated in the photograph is about 5 ft. high.

The monolithic wall at the temple mound is aligned to face exactly south-east. It stands as though built for eternity and may well be the wall of a shrine for the hearts of kings.

278 In contrast to the close-set monolithic wall the two *sides of the temple mound at Ollantaytambo* are covered not with contiguous rectangular blocks but by monoliths separated by flat walls of worked stones held together by a sort of clay mortar. These side-walls could not have been built by the craftsmen responsible for the front wall. The monoliths

are not utilized in the manner for which they were designed. This is obvious in the dissonance between the regular and smoothly finished blocks and the casual filling of the spaces between them; and the point is further brought out by a *T-shaped groove worked in block VIII*. These grooves 279 were intended to enable two blocks to be held together by copper cramps fixed into contiguous slots. The T-groove on the left of block VIII in the south-west wall is pointless, since it lies adjacent to masonry which would not take a cramp. Another well-preserved *groove for a copper cramp* 279 occurs on the edge of a monolith which is lying in front of the temple wall *(274, above)*. This technique is known from the famous ruined site of Pumapunca near Tiahuanaco (to the south-east of Lake Titicaca) where large and regular monoliths were also employed.

The side walls of the Ollantaytambo temple were worked by descendants of the masters. They were familiar with the general plan and attempted to complete the undertaking. But they no longer knew how to handle the monoliths they inherited from their forebears, and were not capable of erecting a wall like that at the front of the temple. Thus the earlier craftsmen who worked the front wall can be distinguished from their successors. But even the work of the latter was not finished, as is shown by monoliths, like that lying in front of the south-west wall *(278)*, which were brought up as far as the temple mound but never utilized.

The question arises what tools the masons of the time had available to cut and finish these great stones and set their angles and corners. Unfortunately scarcely any of these tools have survived. One thing however is certain, that the ancient Peruvians did not have iron tools, since before the arrival of Europeans in America iron was either unknown or was unappreciated. Only copper, and later bronze, was used for working tools. By Inca times a process is said to have been known for hardening copper to an efficiency equivalent to that of forged iron; but it has not yet been possible to find proof of this tradition. Apart from metal implements there were also stone tools. It should never be forgotten that the people of the Andes drew on the experience of over a thousand years of stone working and had a greater knowledge of stone and its possibilities than perhaps any other people in the world. We run the risk of undervaluing a culture which used exclusively copper and stone tools simply because they were not of iron or steel. Copper tools can be extraordinarily well developed and might in some places be preferred to iron for certain qualities, such as freedom from rusting. At all events ancient stone-workers have accomplished masterpieces, like those we have been examining. They moreover sawed stone, and bored through it; both techniques are represented at Ollantaytambo.

The rock fragments which provided the monoliths lie high on the mountain on the other side of the valley. Each monolith, weighing several tons, must have been brought down into the valley and across the river and then transported up the long path to the rocks of the citadel. The greenish schist of the site itself and the rock of the whole surrounding mountain is not suitable for monolithic blocks. These ancient builders did not hesitate to fetch appropriate material even though it lay on the far side of the valley.

280 Certain of the rough-hewn blocks were however left lying along the way. These are the *piedras cansadas, the 'weary stones'*, which are said to have grown so tired along the route they could not finish their journey. The stone in the photograph is 22 ft. long and 7 ft. wide; as accurately as could be measured it is about 2 ft. 9 in. thick. Weighing many tons, it has sunk into the soil like a stranded whale. The rock citadel of Ollantaytambo stands out in the distance above the left end of the stone, light against the darker mountain landscape. This was the goal of the 'weary stone', where it would have found its place had the building been completed.

It must be asked whether the temple citadel of Ollantaytambo is Inca or pre-Inca in date. According to the dates at present accepted for the beginning of the Inca empire, the question would be: was it built before or after 1200? There is no reason to doubt that the terrace walls which divide the hillside into steps are Inca work. If different building techniques can be distinguished, as on the upper north-east terrace, they can be ascribed to different periods of Inca construction. The monolithic work on the temple mound (275–279) would also at present be put in an earlier or later phase of the Inca period. One point here is quite certain, that the monolithic work along the front of the mound (274, 275) is older than the side walls (278). Thus if the front wall is Inca it must date from an earlier part of the Inca period. It is not possible to date it in relation to the list of kings.

By contrast, the position of the uniform megaliths (274, below) on the edge of the upper terrace and in front of the standing monoliths is obscure. The contrast between the handling of megaliths at the Sacsayhuaman and at Ollantaytambo is relevant to this question. The large stones on the temple mound at Ollantaytambo have no counterpart in the Cuzco region, but rather in the slab blocks in the House of the Altar in the ruined city of Machu Picchu (298). But just as we have as yet no conclusive proof that the megalithic element at Sacsayhuaman derives from a pre-Inca period, so are we without proof that the buildings in the Ollantaytambo temple citadel are pre-Inca in date. To give the history of the site in outline: very early the sacred green rocks on the mountain side were ringed round with simple walls containing small trapezoidal niches of no great artistry. Later this simple sanctuary was faced with granite monoliths; the tradition that the Inca buried the entrails of their kings at Ollantaytambo, which speaks for the special importance of the site, would suggest that this work was Inca in date. The nature of the Inca connection with the site is not understood, but because of it the reverse of the monoliths were built up with finely squared stone to face the rather inferior ancient walling, which was nonetheless sacred on account of its altar, and which had particular significance for the Inca, since these ancient and sacred monuments were left unviolated.

It seems improbable that the people of any age would work exclusively in megaliths, in small dressed stones or in rough walling; it is more likely that the purpose of a structure determined the choice of material. But even this dictum is no immutable law of architectural usage. Conclusions should not be modified to fit preconceived ideas. Too rigid a division into megalithic and non-megalithic culture can lead to an unsound judgment. Ollantaytambo also contains numerous buildings in rough-stone walling, a technique which may have lasted from earliest times up till the Spanish conquest. Their classification will be possible only after closer investigation.

The wealth of the Ollantaytambo district is not exhausted by what we have already shown. There are also carved cliffs, like the *Incamisana cliff at Ollantaytambo*. The carvings 281 are nearly 50 ft. high and recall the Kenko and Lacco stones near Cuzco, with the same broad and high vertical surfaces worked in the stone, and the same seats, thrones and altars like intersecting stone rectangles. The worked stone is as smooth as marble. Steps have been cut in the wall on the left to receive squared stone blocks; the rock would have been faced with such blocks. The 'ladder' of steep and very shallow steps on the right in the photograph is a particularly clear example of the footings for a wall which would separate the rock face from various cult chambers.

This explanation has been suggested in connection with the 'steps' on the Lacco rock (258), and it does not conflict with the symbolic character of the rest of the stone carving.

On the far bank of the river Patacancha below the temple
282 citadel lies the *old village of Ollantaytambo* with numerous stone houses and passages dating from Inca times. On the opposite bank, too, at the very foot of the citadel rocks, similar buildings are still standing, as for example the two-storeyed gabled house in the photograph. The door to the lower floor opens in the middle of the long wall. The steps to the upper storey lie outside the house and consist of an open stairway like those built against the facing walls of many cultivation terraces; we find them again at Salapuncu *(288, below)*, set against a wall for easy access.

In the gardens of the Ollantaytambo village under the shade of the trees is a spring called the *baño de la ñusta, the* *283* 'bath of the princess'. The stone, especially in its gently concave curvature, is even more nobly worked than the photograph indicates. The celestial meaning of the setting is expressed in the frame of step symbols. These and the cube-shaped projections (the left-hand one below the first step illuminated by the sunlight) are very similar to the ornamentation of the Choquequilla stone *(262, above)*.

HUAYNA KENTI AND SALAPUNCU

Upstream from Ollantaytambo the Urubamba valley becomes narrower, and its cultivation proportionately more
284 intensive. The great *cultivation terraces* laid out like a map beneath us, supported by walls some 6 ft. high, are the work of Inca times and are still tilled today. The botanical expert with the 1911 Yale expedition, Cook, wrote in admiration of the skill shown in levelling these surfaces; he reported that modern undertakings (in the western United States) sank into insignificance in comparison with what this 'disappearing' race achieved *(Nat. Geog. Mag.,* New York, 1915). The photograph was taken from the *Huayna Kenti,* the 'young humming-bird', an isolated group of ruins lying romantically among re-established thickets at a
285 commanding height above the Urubamba valley. The *trapezoidal gate* was quite overgrown the first time we saw it. Forcing our way through the undergrowth we came upon the ruins, where legend has it that the ñusta, the Inca prin-
286 cess, spent her honeymoon. Among the *Huayna Kenti group is a well-preserved double house* with high gables built of split stone. The niches and parts of the walls still show patches of yellowish-brown, perhaps from painted clay plaster. The two rooms, each 18 ft. by 12 ft., open towards the valley. They are thus really halls. At the base of the gables hollow channels have been left to receive horizontal beams. Each gable wall contains a trapeze-shaped window.
287 Opposite the Huayna Kenti lies the *Nevado Veronica glacier* and its snows in the stillness of the high mountains beneath a sparklingly bright sky. High peaks and especially the snow peaks of the Andes were revered by the mountain peoples and perhaps there was at Huayna Kenti a shrine dedicated to the white mountain opposite. The buildings at Huayna Kenti are overgrown and although they are simpler than other famous ruins they have a greater enchantment.

At first sight *Salapuncu near the bank of the Urubamba* strikes *288* the visitor as the scene of some heroic drama. Everything in Salapuncu is cyclopean, as though made by giants. Entering through a mighty gateway *(288, top right)* one comes on three megalithic zig-zag walls, one above the other, with projecting angles. It is the theme of the Sacsayhuaman which presents itself in a structure which is again related to that site by its monumental stones. The Salapuncu blocks however are not so well dressed, nor are they so tightly fitted together as at Sacsayhuaman. The masonry is coarser though on that very account appears to rise out of its surroundings. Especially in the Salapuncu niches *(288, far left)* do the accumulation of cyclopean stones and the want of artifice reach full expression. If one had to find a match for Salapuncu among the antiquities of the Old World it would be among the buildings of the Hittite capital at Bogazköy. The terrace walls are climbed by means of a *flight of access steps*. The stone steps at Salapuncu are *288* 5 ft. wide, monumental like the rest of the site. I have never ▼ seen such large ones. The *megalithic walls of Salapuncu* are *289* enveloped in the scent of broom, which covers the valley like a sheet of flame. In the distance behind the walls is the mighty back-drop of the snow-covered eastern Cordilleras.

Upstream from Salapuncu the yellow broom intermingles with large lilac-blue umbelliferous flowers, which then come to predominate in the valley. Trees begin to spring up on all sides, first only in the valley bottom but then on the slopes and in the side gullies. The trees become thicker, to form thickets and woods, their tops bending over the light green of the Urubamba river which flows down into the primeval forest.

The river cuts ever deeper into the rock; the valley becomes a gorge. There is room only for the river and the track. The rock walls with their ravines rise almost perpendicular alongside. The billowing vegetation of the green subtropical mountain forest beats together, and orchids bloom.

290 On a ridge above and among the forest lies *Machu Picchu, a city built of white granite*. This name is taken from the mountain on which it lies; its original name is unknown. The city had been completely hidden by the forest until in 1911 it was discovered and cleared by an expedition of the National Geographic Society and Yale University, under the direction of Hiram Bingham. The photograph shows terracing in the foreground, faced with walls of broken stone or polygonal blocks. Behind to the left are the rising ranges of buildings, which Bingham called the 'king's group' and the 'princess's group', with a half-round tower in the centre with two windows, the *Torreón*. To the right of it, on the far side of the 'princess's group', rises a conical mound, the Intihuatana rock *(300)*. In the right background the dark ridge of the Huayna Picchu towers up; there are also walls at its peak.

Separated by a depression from the temple and palace city on the left lies a stepped complex of what may well be secular buildings, which have almost the appearance of a great stepped pyramid. Even in the high Andes the buildings of ancient Peru often appear determined by the basic shape of the pyramid.

291 The *view from the Machu Picchu terraces* is no longer across treeless heights. All the mountains are covered by forest. We have left behind the territory of the highland peasants. Other methods of cultivation prevail in the forests, as is shown by the smoke rising on the opposite side of the valley. The trees must be burnt before the land can be cleared and sown. This is the practice in the Amazon forests. It is difficult to say why the Indians of the highlands established themselves here. Perhaps it was in response to the requirements of the Inca empire for the products of the eastern

forests. Trade routes had to be protected against unruly forest tribes, and this would emphasize the defensive character of the town.

But it should not be forgotten that the city was centred on sanctuaries, about which we know nothing except that they were Inca work, like the rest of the town. The American expedition uncovered exclusively Inca remains, and the trapezoidal doors and windows of Inca (or Cuzco) style are found everywhere.

There must be further ruins undiscovered in the nearby forests. They are spoken of widely, and the descriptions given are often fantastic, but there must be a grain of truth in these reports. The forest regions of the eastern Andean slopes have not yet given up all their secrets to the archaeologist.

Trapezoidal gateways in the 'king's group' at Machu Picchu 292 opening behind each other as in the gallery of a palace. The masonry in ashlar blocks with slightly cushioned faces represents the official Inca building technique no less impressively than the *gateway between the Torreón and the* 293 *'king's group' at Machu Picchu,* leading out into the open. The supporting wall visible through the gateway is in a totally different technique and built from polygonal blocks which, as often in the Cuzco region, are reminiscent of early Greek work, rather as in the supporting wall in the temple of Apollo at Delphi. The wall shown here can also be seen on pl. *296,* rising behind the niche wall.

The *Torreón group at Machu Picchu* is named after a half- 294 round tower *(294, below)* which surrounds a sacred rock. Rising out of a sepulchral cave, the rock has little offering tables carved into its upper surface *(295)*. Thus the tower is not an independent building, but curves in an irregular semicircle around the sacred rock. Its masonry is fitted so precisely, though without mortar, against the natural stone that the two appear continuous.

In its remarkable curve the tower recalls the 'apse' of the temple of the sun at Cuzco *(220)*. The two buildings are without doubt related. I should consider the 'apse' the older building.

The tower window *(294, above)*, aligned to face exactly south-east, reveals in the precision of its stonework the great significance which the tower, the sacred rock and the cave beneath must have had. Its dimensions are: height 2 ft. 6 in., width 16 in. above and 20 in. below, thickness (that of the wall) 2 ft. 2 in. The four projections at the corners of the window serve no practical purpose; they must have had symbolic meaning for the ancients. They recall the projections on the Choquequilla stone in the

Huaracondo gorge (262, above), which were certainly pure symbols.

In the cave below the Torreón rock, too, stone lugs have been inserted between high (4 ft. 6 in.) niches and they are undoubtedly symbolic, though again incomprehensible. Our understanding of the important Peruvian symbolism, alike in design as in sculpture, remains fairly incomplete.

295 The *whole tower rock at Machu Picchu*, lying obliquely over the cave with its altar-like carvings and niches, was no less sacred than the cave itself, which was perhaps a mausoleum. Bingham called the tower complex, together with the connecting walls, 'the group of the king's mausoleum'. At all events this complex, together with the wall with niches in the next plate, must be treated as a unit and only so is it explicable.

296 The light granite *wall with niches near the Torreón at Machu Picchu* was called by its discoverer, Bingham, 'the most beautiful wall in America'. The side facing the tower is a masterpiece of ancient architecture. Its surface is divided by a row of very regular niches, 2 ft. 9 in. high, with a rectangular projection exactly centred between each pair. The purpose or significance of projections in this position is as obscure as with those in the mausoleum cave. On numerous buildings similar projections served to secure the roof. But from finding them in the burial cave we may conclude that they were also installed for quite different reasons.

Behind the wall with niches one sees the support wall of polygonal stones, of which a section was visible through the gateway illustrated in pl. *293*. The contrast between the different modes of construction is particularly obvious in this view.

At the foot of the Intihuatana rock (cf. pl. *290, background*) lies a second centre in the city, a sacred space between 297 temple buildings. One of these buildings is the '*house of the three windows' at Machu Picchu*. Very carefully worked stones of different sizes have been set together to form a window frontage. The block slab which forms the base of the middle window is 6 ft. 6 in. long; the window itself is 4 ft. high. I am assured by widely travelled visitors that the view from these temple windows is among the most splendid not only in Peru but in the whole world. The huge gorge of the Urubamba lies below.

In the background is a range of mountains covered with untouched subtropical forest and rising to heights of over 9,000 ft., with a snow-covered peak of the eastern chain of the Andes, over 15,000 ft. high, rising in the distance beyond.

Large slab-like blocks are also built into the side walls of this temple, reminding us of the monoliths of Ollantaytambo. That site will also come to mind in connection with what Bingham named the *main temple at Machu* 298 *Picchu*, which we may also call the '*house of the altar*' from its gigantic and uniform altar monolith 14 ft. x 5 ft. x 2 ft. 6 in. The front of this temple, like the previous one, is open; they form open temple halls.

The House of the Altar is built with great regularity. One must check the placing of the stones to appreciate this. In the walls of this temple, even more than in those of the House of the Three Windows, there appear great monoliths reminiscent of Ollantaytambo, the work of Inca master-builders of an earlier or later period. They cannot be far removed in time from those who built at that site. The terminal monolith in the left side-wall of the temple (*298*) projects forward; it is 10 ft. 3 in. long, 8 ft. high and 2 ft 6 in. thick. The light-grey granite is wonderfully worked and the outcurving foot of the block is like the pedestal of a statue. The niches recall these at Ollantaytambo and at the Coricancha, the sun temple at Cuzco. A comparative study of niches in the architecture of the Cuzco region and the wider Inca domain is an important task for the future.

Behind the House of the Altar, and between it and the Intihuatána rock, lies the *House of the Priest*. Although 299 smaller, it closely resembles the previous building in its masterly handling of granite blocks and their regular disposition in the wall, as well as in the great beauty of the niches which are here almost more expressive than in the House of the Altar (*298*) or the wall with niches near the Torreón (*296*).

The *Intihuatána rock at Machu Picchu* rises high above the 300 last-named temple (cf. the mound with ruins in the background in pl. *290*). It is approached by steps cut in the natural rock, leading to a small flat space with a rectangular pillar 2 ft. 3 in. high on a wide pedestal in the centre. The pillar and pedestal are carved from the same piece of rock. The pillar stands in a defined relationship to the heavens. In Quechua (the official language of the Inca empire) *Intihuatána* means 'the change from winter to summer', and Middendorf translates *inti huatay* as 'the tethering of the sun, which according to ancient Peruvian belief prevented it from inclining further to the north'. Thus this was the place where the sun was ceremonially secured so

continued on p. 305

259

274

that it would return south and thereby initiate the southern summer. The day when the sun changed direction may have been determined by the shadow cast by such Intihuatána pillars or mounds. But this seems hardly possible. They must rather have been connected with symbolic cult celebrations at the winter solstice, in which the sun was perhaps symbolically fettered and constrained to turn back. The sun god was the most important god of the Inca state and the reigning Inca himself officiated at the *Inti Raymo,* the feast of the winter solstice, which was celebrated in June. This was the cardinal religious feast of the year.

The pedestal is a wonderful example of artistic stonework and it, too, in the spiral line of its flat surface running up to the pillar, is a piece of symbolism carved in stone, which must relate to the great theme of the sun's course. For mountain peoples living many thousands of feet above sea-level the sun must have seemed the god who directed life and work by his movements through the heavens. Looking down from the Intihuatána rock on the *eastern* 301 *part of the city of Machu Picchu* and the mountain forests of the Urubamba gorge.

THE ISLAND OF THE SUN

When the Inca were building Machu Picchu they were working in a climatic and ecological setting which was foreign, not to say hostile, to them. By contrast, when they pushed the boundaries of their empire across Lake Titicaca they were in surroundings which suited them. The lake lies at about 12,000 ft. and is thus not much higher than Cuzco, the residence of the Inca. Moreover the expanse of water in the 120-mile long lake softens the climate, so that even maize can ripen on its banks and islands. The largest of these islands is called the Island of the Sun (Isla del Sol, or sometimes Titicaca island). Already in the oldest, pre-Inca, times it was sacred territory for the Aymará, the inhabitants of the high Andean Collao region around Lake Titicaca. When the Inca occupied the island in the fifteenth century they acknowledged its sanctity They built there in the architectural 'type' style of this century, when the Inca empire was at its apogee. The 302 most important building is the so-called *Inca palace of Pilcocayma* on a terrace on the banks of the Island of the Sun. The Inca Tupac Yupanqui is named as the builder. The Pilcocayma is a two-storey building constructed from stones of different sizes, and originally it was apparently finely plastered and painted, the outer walls in yellow, the gateways, niches and inner walls in red. The inner rooms are *roofed by false vaults*; the walls are corbelled 302 forward and the roof then closed by two long stones. In our photograph we are looking vertically upwards into one of the vaults.

The forward wall of the building is pierced by two trapezoidal gates. The *view through a gateway in the Inca* 303 *palace of Pilcocayma* is one of the most splendid in the Andes. Below is the lake and the dark silhouette of the Island of the Moon; beyond in the distance the high range of the *Cordillera Real,* the royal Cordillera, and the stillness of the white mountains. The height of the eastern Cordillera can be judged from the clearly defined snowline which lies at about 15,000 ft. In the opinion of the American scholar Bandelier the Pilcocayma is dedicated to the highest peak, Illampu, the 'crown of the Andes', and was a shrine for worship of the snow peak which had long been venerated by the people of the mountains. The gateway was set up with this in mind, and not because of the wonderful view or the beauties of nature, which were notions foreign to the people of the time. In ancient Peru, alike in the mountains as on the coast, their constant concern was with their origins, with which the future was involved. We have already encountered this intense respect for places of origin, which are made into shrines, in the case of the sacred rocks and caves of the plateau above Cuzco.

Veneration of origins and of ancestors was no less predominant among the Aymará of the Titicaca uplands, and the Island of the Sun was already sacred on account of their shrines before the Inca brought in legends of their own mythical past and linked it with the appearance of the sun god. In this way the island became one of the most sacred places in the Inca empire. But the holiest of the shrines was the *Titicala rock, near the north-west end of the Island of the Sun*. After the time of darkness the sun had risen from it to form the first day. The rock had been the house of the sun (Bernabé Coco, IV, 55). In legend the sun god had long been related to the family of the ruling Inca. 'Our father, the sun god', he was ceremonially called by the Inca himself. The sun god sent forth two of his children, Manco Capac, the first Inca, and his wife, Mama Ocllo (Garcilasso de la Vega, II). Leaving the Island of the Sun and the sacred rock they travelled to the high valleys of the north-west. In sight of the Cuzco valley on the Huanacauri mountain Manco Capac thrust a golden staff into the ground. The staff sank into the ground and Manco Capac remained to found Cuzco and, with it, the Inca empire. According to Garcilasso all the later Inca kings descended from these wanderers. Thus in the beliefs of the Inca people the Titicaca rock was the starting-point for the great historical development of ancient Peru. Pilgrims could approach it only after confession and penitence, and then only to the edge of the level ground in front of the rock. Only members of the Inca's family and priests were allowed to approach it. As a shrine the rock may have been coated with gold and silver and covered with splendidly coloured textiles of vicuña wool. So must the rocky hump have appeared to the worshippers, adorned for display like something wonderful from fable and legend. Much of what had meaning and colour for the ancient peoples will pale in the cool light of historical examination. Not everything, however, was fable or mythical belief. Behind the legend about Manco Capac and the sun god could be concealed connections between Cuzco and the Titicaca region, which includes the ruined site of Tiahuanaco with its many unsolved problems. The connections would relate to the origin of the Inca. Many archaeological observations are consistent with migration of a tribe and a culture from the Titicaca lake to the high valleys of the Cuzco region. The Titicala rock, even in its present form deprived of ceremonial trappings, could then be regarded as a symbol of the migration of men as much as of the ideas of past and credulous ages.

304

My own photographs were supplemented by material from the following sources, and I wish to express my grateful thanks to the owners: 37, 39 and 53 were made available by the Servicio Aereofotográfico Nacional de Peru; 58–61, 63, 66–69, 72–74, 76–89, 91, 92 (left) 93, (below), 94 (left), 95, 97, 100, 101, 108 (below), 110–113, 117–123, 125–127, 129, 132–136, 150, 154–157, 174, 175, 177–179, 182–187, 188 (below), 189, 201, 272 by R. Braunmüller, Museum für Völkerkunde, Munich; 101, 102 by W. Hecker; 152, 153 by Frau Caecilie Seler-Sachs.

BIBLIOGRAPHY

Bandelier, A. F., *The islands of Titicaca and Koati* (New York, 1910).

Bennett, W. C., 'Chavín stone carving', in *Anthropological Studies*, 3 (Yale University, New Haven, 1942).

Bennett, W. C., 'The North Highlands of Peru, Excavations in the Callejón de Huaylas and at Chavín de Huantar', *Anthropological Papers of the American Museum of Natural History*, Vol. 39, Part I (New York, 1944).

Bennett, W. C., 'The archeology of the Central Andes', *Bulletin, Bureau of American Ethnology*, 143, 1946, vol. 2.

Bennett, W. C. and Bird, J. B., *Andean Culture History* (New York, 1949).

Bennett, W. C., *The Gallinazo group Virú valley, Peru*, Yale University Publications in Anthropology, 43 (New Haven, 1950).

Bennett, W. C., *Ancient Arts of the Andes*, The Museum of Modern Art (New York, 1954).

Bingham, H., 'In the wonderland of Perú', *National Geographic Magazine*. 24, 1913, pp. 387–573.

Bingham, H., *Machu Picchu, a citadel of the Incas* (New Haven, 1930).

Bird, J. B. and Bellinger, L., *Paracas fabrics and Nazca needlework* (The Textile Museum, Washington, D. C., 1954).

Cieza de León, P. de, *Parte Primera de la chronica del Perú* (Antwerp, 1554).

Cobo, B., *Historia del Nuevo Mundo*, ed. Marcos Jiménez de la Espada (Seville, 1890–95).

Collier, D., *El desarollo de la civilización peruana* (Bogotá, 1959).

Disselhoff, H. D., *Die Kunst der Andenländer* in H. D. Disselhoff and Sigvald Linné, *Alt-Amerika* (Baden-Baden, 1960).

Doering, H. U., 'Tonplastik aus Nazca', IPEK, 2, 1927, pp. 167–75.

Doering, H. U., *Altperuanische Gefäßmalereien*, Part I: Marburger Jahrbuch für Kunstwissenschaft, ed. Richard Hamann und Hans Weigert, vol. 2, 1925/26, pp. 1–70 (Marburg/Lahn, Verlag des Kunstwissenschaftl. Seminars der Universität); and Part II, vol. 6, 1931, pp. 1–63.

Doering, H. U., *The Art of Ancient Peru* (New York, 1952).

Doering, H. U., 'Bericht über archäologische Feldarbeiten in Perú' (Nazcaregion, south Peru; 1932), *Ethnos*, 1958, 2–4; Bericht II (Pacatnamú; Cupisnique; 1937–39), *Ethnos*, 1959, 1–2; Bericht III (Pacatnamú; Tecapa and Jatanca; 1953/54), *Ethnos*, 1960, 3–4.

Engel, F., Notes relatives à des explorations archéologiques à Paracas et sur la côte sud du Pérou', in *Travaux de l'Institut Français d'Etudes Andines*, vol. IX (Paris-Lima, 1963).

Harcourt, R. d', *Les textiles anciens du Pérou el leurs techniques,* (Paris, 1934).

Harcourt, R. d' (ed. by Grace G. Denny and Carolyn M. Osborne), *Textiles of Ancient Peru and their techniques* (Seattle, 1962).

Horkheimer, *El Peru Prehispánico* (Lima, 1950).

Horkheimer, H., 'Nahrung und Nahrungsgewinnung im vorspanischen Perú', in *Bibliotheca Ibero-Americana*, vol. II (Berlin, 1960).

Joyce, T. A., *South American Archaeology* (Boston, Mass., 1912).

Kaiser, W., 'Stand und Probleme der ägyptischen Vorgeschichtsforschung', *Zeitschrift für Ägyptische Sprache und Altertumskunde*, vol. 81 (Berlin, 1956).

Kinzl, H., 'Die Dünen in der Küstenlandschaft von Perú', in *Mitteilungen der Geographischen Gesellschaft in Wien*, vol. 100, I/II, 1958.

Krickeberg, W., *Felsplastik und Felsbilder bei den Kulturvölkern Altamerikas* (Berlin, 1949).

Kroeber, A. L., *Peruvian Archeology in 1942*, Viking Fund Publications in Anthropology, 4 (New York, 1944).

Kroeber, A. L., 'Toward definition of the Nazca style', in *Publications in American Archaeology and Ethnology*, vol. 43, No. 4, pp. 327–432 (University of California, Berkeley, 1956).

Kroeber, A. L., *Art*, Bulletin 143, Smithsonian Institution, Washington, D. C., vol. 5, pp. 411–492.

Larco Hoyle, R., *Los Cupisiniques* (Lima, 1941).

Larco Hoyle, R., *Cronología Arqueológica del Norte del Perú* (Buenos Aires, 1946).

Lothrop, S. K., *Altamerikanische Kunst* (Olten and Freiburg, 1959).

Means, P. A., *Ancient Civilizations of the Andes* (New York, 1931).

Middendorf, E. W., *Perú*, II, 'Das Küstenland von Perú' (Berlin, 1894); III, 'Das Hochland von Perú' (Berlin, 1895).

Mujica Gallo, M., *Gold in Peru* (Recklinghausen, 1959).

Nordenskiöld, E., *The copper and bronze ages in South America* (Göteborg, 1946).

O'Neale, L. M., in 'Textiles of the Early Nazca period', *Anthropology Memoirs*, Field Museum of Natural History, 2, 1937, no. 3.

O'Neale, L. M., 'Textile periods in ancient Peru', in *Publications in American Archaeology and Ethnology*, vol. 39, no. 2 (1942), and vol. 40, no. 4 (1948); (University of California, Berkeley).

Rowe, J. H., 'An introduction to the archaeology of Cuzco' (Papers of the Peabody Museum of American Archaeology and Ethnology, Harvard University), vol. XXVI, no. 2 (Cambridge, Mass., 1944).

Rowe, J. H., 'The Kingdom of Chimor', in *Acta Americana*, 6, 1948, pp. 26–59.

Rowe, J. H., *Chavín Art* (The Museum of Primitive Art, New York, 1962).

Schmidt, M., 'Über altperuanische Gewebe mit szenenhaften Darstellungen', *Baessler-Archiv*, I, 1910.

Schmidt, M., *Kunst und Kultur von Perú* (Berlin, 1929).

Schmoekel, H., *Das Land Sumer* (Stuttgart, 1956).

Strong, W. D. and Evans, C., 'Cultural stratigraphy in the Virú valley, northern Perú', *Columbia Studies in Archaeology and Ethnology*, 4, (New York, 1952).

Squier, E. G., *Perú* (Leipzig, 1883).

Tello, J. C., *Origen y desarollo de las civilizaciones prehistóricas andinas* (Lima, 1942).

Tello, J. C., 'Discovery of the Chavín culture in Peru', in *American Antiquity*, 9, 1943, pp. 136–160.

Trimborn, H., *Das Alte Amerika* (Stuttgart, 1959).

Troll, C., 'Die geographischen Grundlagen des Inca-Reiches', in *Ibero-Amerikanisches Archiv*, V/3 (Berlin, n. d.).

Valcarcel, L. E., 'Sajsahuaman redescubierto', in *Revista*, Museo Nacional de Lima, 3, 1934, pp. 3–36; and 'Los trabajos arqueológicos del Cusco', ibid., pp. 211–223.

Woolley, L. *Ur of the Chaldees* (1930).